# PHILIP'S

# Cycle TOURS

# Around London South

## Nick Cotton

First published in 2002 by
Philip's, a division of
Octopus Publishing Group Ltd
2-4 Heron Quays
London E14 4JP

First edition 2002
Third impression 2007

Based on the original Ordnance Survey Cycle Tours series
first published by Philip's and Ordnance Survey®.

ISBN-10  0-540-08193-0
ISBN-13  978-0-540-08193-6

The route maps in this book are reproduced from
Ordnance Survey® Landranger® mapping.

Text and compilation copyright © Philip's 2002

Ordnance Survey®

**Photographic acknowledgements**

AA Photo Library 7, 13 • Nick Cotton 107, 119, 123
Graham Todd 67 • Judy Todd 73 top
Andy Williams 19, 31, 43, 49, 73, 97

# Contents

# Abbreviations and symbols

## Directions

| | |
|---|---|
| L | left |
| R | right |
| LH | left-hand |
| RH | right-hand |
| SA | straight ahead or straight across |
| T-j | T-junction, a junction where you have to give way |
| X-roads | crossroads, a junction where you may or may not have to give way |
| 'Placename 2' | words in quotation marks are those that appear on signposts; the numbers indicate distance in miles unless stated otherwise |

## Distance and grade

The number of drink bottles indicates the grade:

🍶 Easy
🍶🍶🍶 Moderate
🍶🍶🍶🍶🍶 Strenuous

The grade is based on the amount of climbing involved.

## Refreshments

Pubs and teashops on or near the route are listed. The tankard ♥ symbols indicate pubs particularly liked by the author.

# Page diagrams

The page diagrams on the introductory pages show how the map pages have been laid out, how they overlap and if any inset maps have been used.

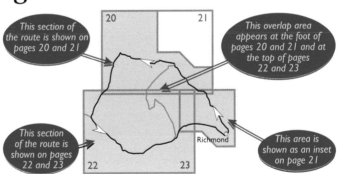

This section of the route is shown on pages 20 and 21

This overlap area appears at the foot of pages 20 and 21 and at the top of pages 22 and 23

This section of the route is shown on pages 22 and 23

This area is shown as an inset on page 21

Richmond

20     21     22     23

# Cross-profiles

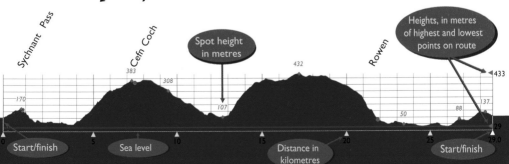

Sychnant Pass

Cefn Coch

Spot height in metres

Rowen

Heights, in metres of highest and lowest points on route

170   383   308   107   432   50   88   137   433   29

Start/finish    Sea level    Distance in kilometres    Start/finish

0   5   10   15   20   25   29.0

# Legend to 1:50 000 maps

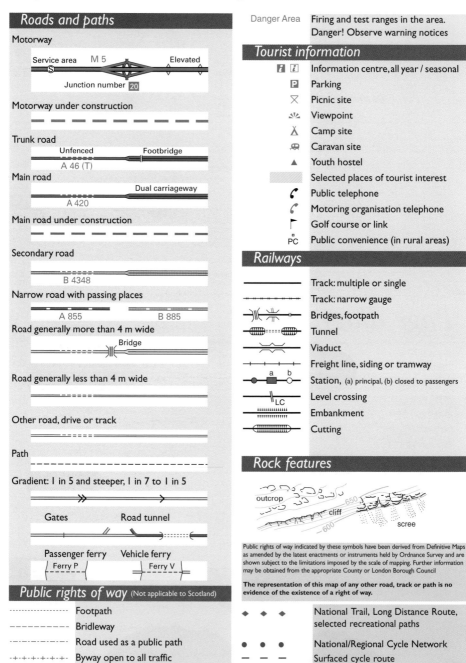

## Roads and paths

**Motorway**

Service area — M 5 — Elevated
Junction number — 20

**Motorway under construction**

**Trunk road**
Unfenced — Footbridge
A 46 (T)

**Main road**
Dual carriageway
A 420

**Main road under construction**

**Secondary road**
B 4348

**Narrow road with passing places**
A 855 — B 885

**Road generally more than 4 m wide**
Bridge

**Road generally less than 4 m wide**

**Other road, drive or track**

**Path**

**Gradient: 1 in 5 and steeper, 1 in 7 to 1 in 5**

Gates — Road tunnel

Passenger ferry — Vehicle ferry
Ferry P — Ferry V

## Public rights of way (Not applicable to Scotland)

·············· Footpath
– – – – – – Bridleway
–·–·–·–·– Road used as a public path
–+–+–+–+– Byway open to all traffic

Danger Area — Firing and test ranges in the area. Danger! Observe warning notices

## Tourist information

🅸 🅘 Information centre, all year / seasonal
🅿 Parking
✕ Picnic site
� Viewpoint
⋏ Camp site
🚐 Caravan site
▲ Youth hostel
▨ Selected places of tourist interest
✆ Public telephone
✆ Motoring organisation telephone
⌐ Golf course or link
PC Public convenience (in rural areas)

## Railways

Track: multiple or single
Track: narrow gauge
Bridges, footpath
Tunnel
Viaduct
Freight line, siding or tramway
a b Station, (a) principal, (b) closed to passengers
LC Level crossing
Embankment
Cutting

## Rock features

outcrop — 650 — cliff — 600 — scree

Public rights of way indicated by these symbols have been derived from Definitive Maps as amended by the latest enactments or instruments held by Ordnance Survey and are shown subject to the limitations imposed by the scale of mapping. Further information may be obtained from the appropriate County or London Borough Council

**The representation of this map of any other road, track or path is no evidence of the existence of a right of way.**

◆ ◆ ◆ National Trail, Long Distance Route, selected recreational paths

● ● ● National/Regional Cycle Network
– – – Surfaced cycle route

4

## Water features

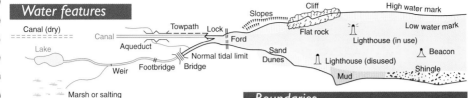

Canal (dry)

Canal

Lake

Aqueduct

Towpath Lock

Ford

Weir Footbridge Bridge

Normal tidal limit

Marsh or salting

Slopes Cliff High water mark

Flat rock Low water mark

Lighthouse (in use)

Sand

Dunes Lighthouse (disused) Beacon

Mud Shingle

## General features

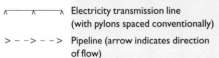 Electricity transmission line
(with pylons spaced conventionally)

> - -> - -> Pipeline (arrow indicates direction of flow)

 Buildings

Public buildings (selected)

 Bus or coach station

Coniferous wood

Non-coniferous wood

Mixed wood

Orchard

Park or ornamental grounds

Quarry

Spoil heap, refuse tip or dump

Ⱦ Radio or TV mast

Church or chapel with tower

Church or chapel with spire

+ Church or chapel without tower or spire

○ Chimney or tower

Glasshouse

+ Graticule intersection at 5' intervals

Ⓗ Heliport

△ Triangulation pillar

Ⱦ Windmill with or without sails

Ⱦ Windpump

## Boundaries

+ — + — + National

-○- -○- -○- -○- -○- London borough

National park or forest park

NT National Trust   NT open access

NT limited access

—··—·—·— County, region or islands area

+ + + + + District

## Abbreviations

P Post office

PH Public house

MS Milestone

MP Milepost

CH Clubhouse

PC Public convenience (in rural areas)

TH Town hall, guildhall or equivalent

CG Coastguard

## Antiquities

VILLA Roman

Castle Non-Roman

⤬ Battlefield (with date)

☆ Tumulus

+ Position of antiquity which cannot be drawn to scale

ℳ Ancient monuments and historic buildings in the care of the Secretaries of State for the Environment, for Scotland and for Wales and that are open to the public

## Heights

═══50═══ Contours are at 10 metres vertical interval

·144 Heights are to the nearest metre above mean sea level

Heights shown close to a triangulation pillar refer to the station height at ground level and not necessarily to the summit

# A ring around Basingstoke from Old Basing

This is prosperous agricultural country with rolling fields of arable farmland forming the backdrop to much of the ride. Small areas of woodlands with broadleaf deciduous trees give an indication of the chalk and clay geology and soil. The route describes a loop around Basingstoke, to avoid the dual carriageways and ring roads that make it a better town for driving rather than cycling.

8    9

Basingstoke   Old Basing

10    11

 **Start**

St Mary's Church, Old Basing, 3 km (2 miles) east of Basingstoke.

**P** No specific car park. Some spaces near church. Alternatively, park in the car park for Basing House (follow signs) and return to church

 **Distance and grade**

61 km (38 miles)

Easy

**Terrain**

Gently undulating ride, flatter in the northern section. No serious climbs. Lowest point – 50 m (165 ft) at crossing of River Loddon near Stratfield Saye. Highest point – 176 m (580 ft) at Herriard, east of Axford

**Nearest railway**

Bramley, on the route (instruction 10). Hook (east of the route at Newnham (instruction 3)

  **Refreshments**

Millstone PH 🍴, Crown PH, Bolton Arms PH, **Old Basing**
Old House at Home PH, **Newnham**
Coach & Horses PH 🍴🍴, **Rotherwick** *(just off the route)*
Fox PH, **Lyde Green**
New Inn PH 🍴, **Stratfield Saye**
Swan PH, **Sherborne St John**
Fox PH, Barley Mow PH, **East Oakley**
Wheatsheaf Hotel , **North Waltham**
Queen PH 🍴🍴, **Dummer** *(off the route, near North Waltham)*

Old Basing    Newnham    Stratfield Saye    Bramley    Sherborne St John

130
80    90    90    80    70    80

0    5    10    15    20    25    30

### Basing House 1

A ruined house, once the largest private house in Tudor England, it was destroyed by Cromwell's troops in 1645. An exhibition in the 19th-century Lodge House explains the history

▲ All Saints' Church, Dummer

### The Vyne 11/12

Three wings form an E-shaped Tudor mansion, set by a lake adjoining River Loddon. Among the best features of the house are the Gothic antechapel, the chapel itself, with fine Flemish stained glass and Italian glazed floor tiles, the sunny oak gallery and the neoclassical hall and staircase decorated in pale blue and white

### Dummer (just off the route near North Waltham)

All Saints' Church is located near the crossroad at the end of the Main Street. It is listed in the Domesday Book, but the oldest visible part is the 12th-century doorway of the nave. Described by Sir John Betjeman as having 'rustic cottagey interest', this small church has a number of notable features including one of the few virtually intact medieval rood canopies, a gallery and one of the oldest pulpits in the country (1380). The Old Rectory, a magnificent 19th-century flint and stone building, stands opposite the church, many times its size

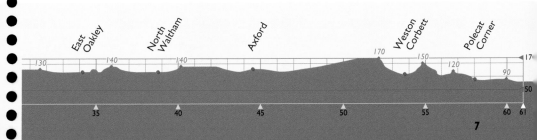

**1** With back to the church, opposite Siege and Brook Cottages, turn R to go under railway bridge

**2** After 1 km (¾ mile), towards the end of Old Basing, turn R by triangle of grass onto Newnham Lane 'Newnham'

**3** After 4 km (2½ miles) at X-roads by telephone box in Newnham, L onto Ridge Lane 'Rotherwick, Hartley Wespall'

**4** After 4 km (2½ miles) and shortly after the signpost at start of Hartley Wespall village and immediately after triangle of grass and bus shelter on left, next R 'Turgis Green 1½'

**5** At T-j with a long red brick wall to the left R 'Chandlers Green 1, Mattingley 2¾', then (**easy to miss**) shortly 1st L (NS)

**6** At X-roads with A33 by Wellington Arms Hotel SA (**take care** – busy road) 'Stratfield Saye 1¾'

**7** Shortly after crossing bridge over river, on sharp RH bend, 1st L 'Stratfield Saye, Bramley'

**8** At X-roads in Stratfield Saye by the New Inn PH L 'Bramley'

**9** SA through X-roads following signs for Bramley Station

**10** At T-j at the end of Bramley Lane R over railway crossing 'Sherborne St John 3½, Basingstoke 7'

**11** After 2 km (1¼ miles) shortly after No Through Road sign and Parish Church to the right, next L 'Sherborne St John 2½, Basingstoke 6'

**12** In Sherborne St John 1st R after the Swan PH onto Cranes Road 'Monk Sherborne, Aldermaston'

**13** At T-j with A340 R 'Monk Sherborne 1' then 1st L (same sign)

**14** Shortly after Monk Sherborne village sign, on sharp RH bend by triangle of grass with memorial cross, turn L

**15** At X-roads with the busy A339 (take care) SA 'Wootton St Lawrence'

**16** At T-j R 'Wootton St Lawrence ½, Oakley 3½'

**17** At T-j L 'Newfound 1½, Oakley 3'

**18** At T-j with B3400 R 'Whitchurch 8½', then 1st L by the Fox PH onto Fox Lane 'Oakley 1½'

➡ **three pages**

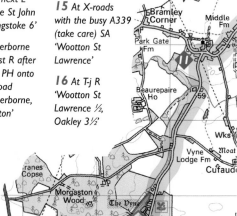

**29** At X-roads (with A30) by petrol station SA onto Byfleet Avenue

**30** At traffic lights SA onto Milkingpen Lane 'Newnham ½' then 2nd L opposite St Mary's primary school onto Church Lane

**31** At the church, dismount and walk through the churchyard to return to the start

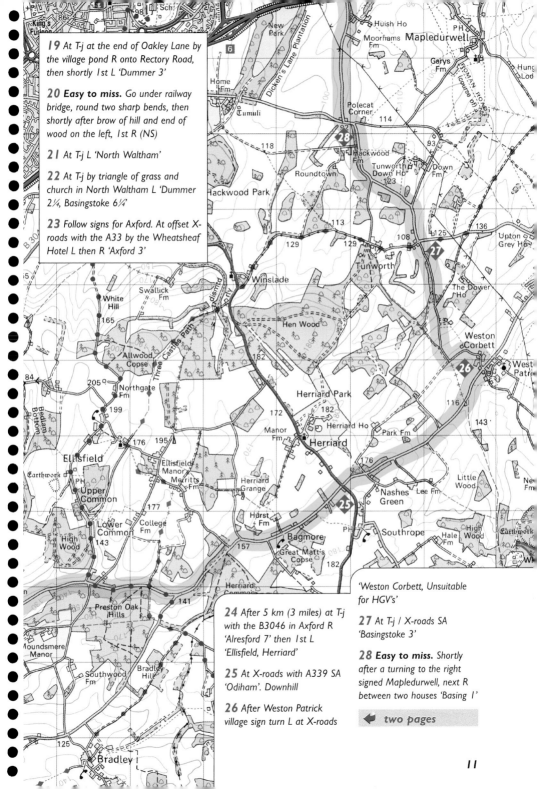

**19** At T-j at the end of Oakley Lane by the village pond R onto Rectory Road, then shortly 1st L 'Dummer 3'

**20 Easy to miss.** Go under railway bridge, round two sharp bends, then shortly after brow of hill and end of wood on the left, 1st R (NS)

**21** At T-j L 'North Waltham'

**22** At T-j by triangle of grass and church in North Waltham L 'Dummer 2¼, Basingstoke 6¼'

**23** Follow signs for Axford. At offset X-roads with the A33 by the Wheatsheaf Hotel L then R 'Axford 3'

**24** After 5 km (3 miles) at T-j with the B3046 in Axford R 'Alresford 7' then 1st L 'Ellisfield, Herriard'

**25** At X-roads with A339 SA 'Odiham'. Downhill

**26** After Weston Patrick village sign turn L at X-roads

'Weston Corbett, Unsuitable for HGV's'

**27** At T-j / X-roads SA 'Basingstoke 3'

**28 Easy to miss.** Shortly after a turning to the right signed Mapledurwell, next R between two houses 'Basing 1'

◀ two pages

# 2 Pines, heathland and quiet Hampshire lanes, south from Farnham

**Start**

Coach & Horses PH, at the bottom of Castle Street, Farnham

P Follow signs

**Distance and grade**

54 km (34 miles)

Easy/moderate

**Terrain**

Generally undulating. Short, steep climb near start through Moor Park east of Farnham. Steady 97 m (320 ft) climb south from Elstead. 82 m (270 ft) climb north from

Crossing parts of both Surrey and Hampshire this ride shows the remarkable difference in population density between the two counties. The exit from Farnham takes you via the highly prosperous residences of Moor Park and parallel with the Hogs Back to the pretty villages of Puttenham and Shackleford. Pines and bracken dominate on the sandy, well-drained soil of the Greensand Beds, spreading across the open heathland of the commons of Crooksbury, Hankley and Ockley, the last two on either side of the road south from Elstead. After leaving the Elstead road near Pitch Place, you are plunged into a series of tiny, little used lanes that, with the exception of three short sections in Churt, Kingsley and Bentley, will lead you for almost 29 km (18 miles) back to Farnham. The landscape turns from heathland to arable farmland and becomes much less built-up in character. After climbing up onto the ridge north of Bentley, the route enters Farnham via broad, good quality, stone-based bridleways that should be passable by all bikes in summer and all but the lightest touring bikes in the winter. A road alternatve down Crondall Lane is also described.

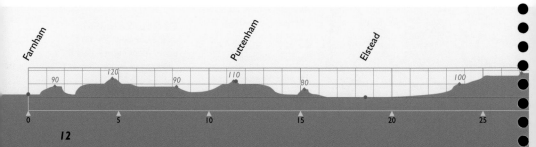

Bentley. Lowest point –
50 m (165 ft) crossing
the River Wey east of
Elstead. Highest point
– 161 m (530 ft) on
the ridge north of
Bentley

### Nearest railway

Farnham Station, on
the route

### Refreshments

Plenty of choice in **Farnham**
Manor Farm Craft Centre Tea Room, **Seale**
Good Intent PH, Jolly Farmer PH 🍴,
**Puttenham**
Cider House Inn 🍴, **Shackleford**
Star PH, Woolpack PH 🍴🍴, **Elstead**
Cedars PH 🍴, **Binsted**
Bull PH 🍴🍴, **Bentley**

### Places of interest

**Farnham** 1
Tudor and Georgian houses flank the 12th-
century Norman castle. The keep is open
to the public. The town museum has
reminders of 17th- and 18th-century life.
To the east, lies the Hog's Back, a 152 m
(500 ft) chalk ridge overlooking the North
Downs Way

**Thursley** 13/14 (just off the route)
A tiny village in the middle of a huge
common. A wild nature reserve includes
woodland, heath and bog. Birds include the
Dartford warbler, and occasionally
Montagu's harrier, merlin, osprey and pere-
grine

**Frensham** 19 (just off the route)
The Great Pond is one of the
largest lakes in southern
England, good for sailing,
fishing and birdwatching. Good
views from the hills known as
the Devil's Jumps

▼ Thutsley Common

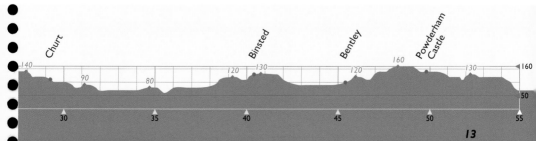

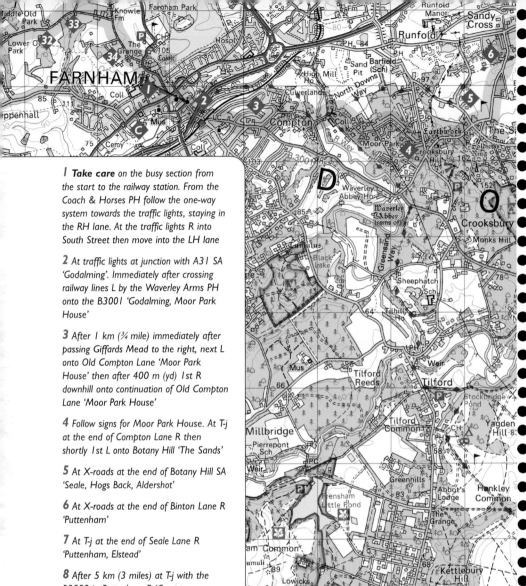

**1** **Take care** on the busy section from the start to the railway station. From the Coach & Horses PH follow the one-way system towards the traffic lights, staying in the RH lane. At the traffic lights R into South Street then move into the LH lane

**2** At traffic lights at junction with A31 SA 'Godalming'. Immediately after crossing railway lines L by the Waverley Arms PH onto the B3001 'Godalming, Moor Park House'

**3** After 1 km (¾ mile) immediately after passing Giffards Mead to the right, next L onto Old Compton Lane 'Moor Park House' then after 400 m (yd) 1st R downhill onto continuation of Old Compton Lane 'Moor Park House'

**4** Follow signs for Moor Park House. At T-j at the end of Compton Lane R then shortly 1st L onto Botany Hill 'The Sands'

**5** At X-roads at the end of Botany Hill SA 'Seale, Hogs Back, Aldershot'

**6** At X-roads at the end of Binton Lane R 'Puttenham'

**7** At T-j at the end of Seale Lane R 'Puttenham, Elstead'

**8** After 5 km (3 miles) at T-j with the B3000 in Puttenham R 'Compton, Godalming', then shortly after the Jolly Farmer PH R again 'Norney'

**9** Shortly after the start of Shackleford 1st R onto Lombard Street 'Cutmill'

**10** **Easy to miss.** After 2 km (1¼ mile) 1st L by small triangle of grass 'Elstead'

**11** At T-j by small triangle of grass R 'Elstead, Farnham'

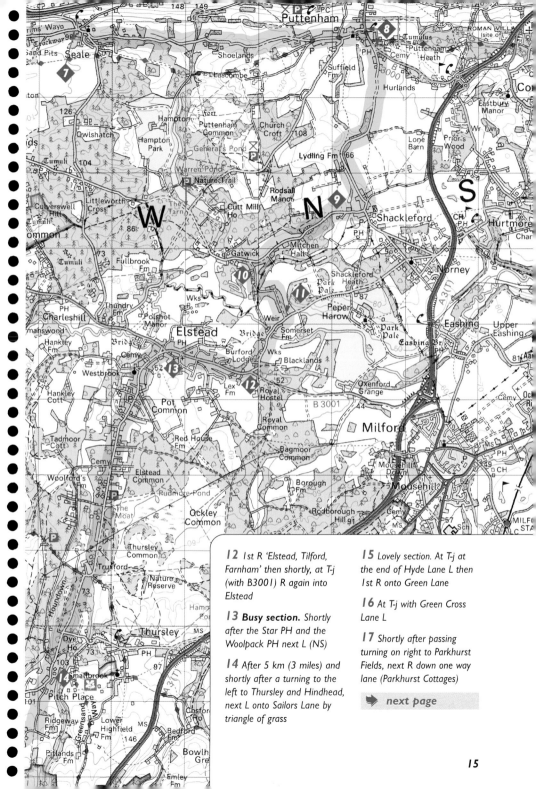

**12** *1st R 'Elstead, Tilford, Farnham' then shortly, at T-j (with B3001) R again into Elstead*

**13** **Busy section.** *Shortly after the Star PH and the Woolpack PH next L (NS)*

**14** *After 5 km (3 miles) and shortly after a turning to the left to Thursley and Hindhead, next L onto Sailors Lane by triangle of grass*

**15** *Lovely section. At T-j at the end of Hyde Lane L then 1st R onto Green Lane*

**16** *At T-j with Green Cross Lane L*

**17** *Shortly after passing turning on right to Parkhurst Fields, next R down one way lane (Parkhurst Cottages)*

➡ *next page*

**16** At T-j with Green Cross Lane L

**17** Shortly after passing turning on right to Parkhurst Fields, next R down one-way lane (Parkhurst Cottages)

**18** At T-j with the A287 by telephone box bear R. Past garage and 2nd telephone box. At brow of hill L onto Lampard Lane 'Simonstone, Wishanger' then 1st L onto Simonstone Lane 'Simonstone'

**19** At X-roads at top of hill SA onto Wishanger Lane

**20** At T-j at the end of Wishanger Lane L onto Frensham Lane 'Headley 2¼, Bordon 3½'

**21** After 1 km (¾ mile), on sharp LH bend, 1st R 'Dockenfield 2, Alton 7½'

**22** At T-j (with stream ahead) turn R (NS)

**23** At offset X-roads with busy A325 L then R onto B3004 'Alton 6, Kingsley 1'

**24 Busy section.** Shortly after start of Kingsley 1st R onto Sickles Lane 'Wheatley 1¼, Binsted 2½ then after 1 km (¾ mile) 1st L 'South Hay'

**25** Secluded stretch. At T-j R (NS)

**26** At X-roads SA 'Isington 1, Bentley 2½'

**27** Easy to miss. In Isington take the 2nd L opposite black and white timbered house called Eggars Cottage 'Froyle 2, Alton 5'

**28** Follow road round to the right and under A31 dual carriageway. At T-j R 'Bentley 1¼, Bentley Station 1¾'

**29** In Bentley, 1st L by the Memorial Hall 'Well 2½, Crondall 4'

**30** Follow signs for Crondall round sharp RH and LH bends. At X-roads R 'Dippenhall 2¼, Farnham 3¾'

**31** (Good-quality, off-road section). At T-j by triangle of grass R 'Dippenhall ½, Farnham 2' then 1st L onto Doras Green Lane. Shortly, on sharp LH bend (chevrons) bear R (in effect SA) 'Lower Old Park' 'Public Bridleway'

**Alternative Route**

**A** Ignore 1st R signposted Bentley. Take 2nd R by triangle of grass 'Dippenhall ¾, Farnham 2¼'

**B** Follow road to the left by triangle of grass in Dippenhall then at T-j opposite craft workshops R (NS)

**C** At T-j in Farnham at the end of Crondall Lane L towards town centre to return to start

**32** Shortly after the brow of the hill, where the tarmac swings sharp left, continue SA downhill on broad track

**33** At T-j of tracks by brick pillars and metal gate by Woodside Cottages, bear R (in effect SA) on continuation of broad track

**34** If there is any mud, the next 300 m (yd) is likely to be the worst section. At T-j with tarmac R. At T-j at the end of Old Park Lane R downhill to return to the start.

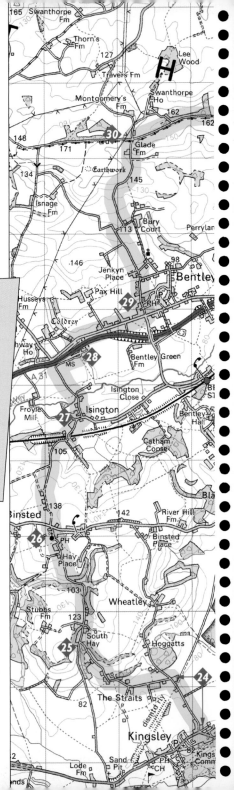

# From Cranleigh through the woods to Gomshall and west to Chiddingfold

**3**

Lovely woodland, quiet lanes and old villages make this one of the best areas close to southwest London for cycling in real countryside. The first climb, through the woods north of Cranleigh, is fairly unforgiving, but the woodland is very beautiful and it is at the start of the ride! Fine refreshment stop at Gomshall Mill and several pubs along the way at Hascombe, Hambledon, Chidding fold and Dunsfold. The route manages to avoid busy roads almost entirely, making use at one point of a paved bridleway west of the A281.

## Start

Stocklund Square, by the clock and fountain, Cranleigh

**P** Follow signs

## Distance and grade

59 km (37 miles)

Moderate/strenuous

## Terrain

A steep climb (almost 183 m (600 ft) from Cranleigh to Winterfold Wood and a shorter, 70 m (230 ft) hill from Brook to Farley Heath. Lots of short, sharp climbs between Shamley Green and Dunsfold

## Nearest railway

Gomshall or Witley, 2½ km (1½ miles) west of Hambledon

## Refreshments

Lots of choice in **Cranleigh**
Compass Inn PH, Gomshall Mill for coffee and tea, **Gomshall** White Horse Inn ●●, Prince of Wales PH, **Shere** William IV PH ●●, **Albury Heath**
White Horse PH ●●, **Hascombe** (just off the route)
Merry Harriers PH ●, **Hambledon**
Swan PH ●●, Crown PH ● (tea is also available), **Chiddingfold** Sun PH ●, **Dunsfold**

### Shere 8

Said to be Surrey's prettiest village, Shere consists of timbered houses and cottages built along the willow-covered banks of a stream. The church is notable for its octagonal spire and

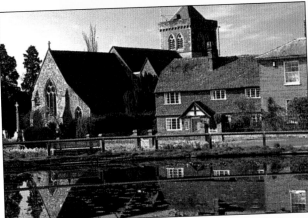

Norman tower. Among the many well-preserved old buildings, the Oak Cottage and the White Horse Inn are of particular interest.

### Winkworth Arboretum 18-19

95 acres of hillside woodland gardens with rare shrubs and trees and two lakes.

### Hascombe 19-20

Lying in a valley between wooded hills, this village is full of attractive, old

▲ *Chiddingfold*

cottages. One of the surrounding ridges, Telegraph Hill, was used as a signalling station during the Napoleonic Wars.

### Oakhurst Cottage, Hambledon 22

This 16th-century, timber-framed cottage has been restored and furnished authentically.

### Chiddingfold 23

An important centre for glass until the 16th century, this village has records of the earliest glass blower, Lawrence, in 1227. The Church of St Mary, overlooking the central green, has only one window of Chiddingfold glass but is interesting nevertheless. Opposite the church is the Crown Inn, one of the oldest inns in the country; it was built as a rest home for Cistercian Monks and became an inn in 1383.

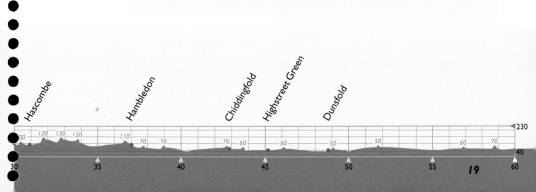

**1** With your back to the fountain R along High Street. At roundabout by obelisk L on Ewhurst Road 'Ewhurst 2, Ockley 6'

**2** After 1 km (¾ mile), opposite telephone box L on Barhatch Lane 'Albury 6, Shere 5'

➡ **two pages**

**19** At T-j with B2130 L 'Hascombe, Dunsfold', then 1st R on Mare Lane '6ft 6ins width limit' (or SA for the White Horse PH)

**20** Steep climb then descent. At T-j at bottom of hill by triangle of grass R (NS)

**21** At X-roads L 'Hambledon, Chiddingfold'

**22** Ignore 1st left to Hambledon Church, take next L opposite house called Bryony Hill 'Pockford, Dunsfold', then at T-j L (NS)

**23** After 5 km (3 miles), at T-j in Chiddingfold R for pubs (tea also available in Crown), shop and village green, or L on Pickhurst Road to continue route

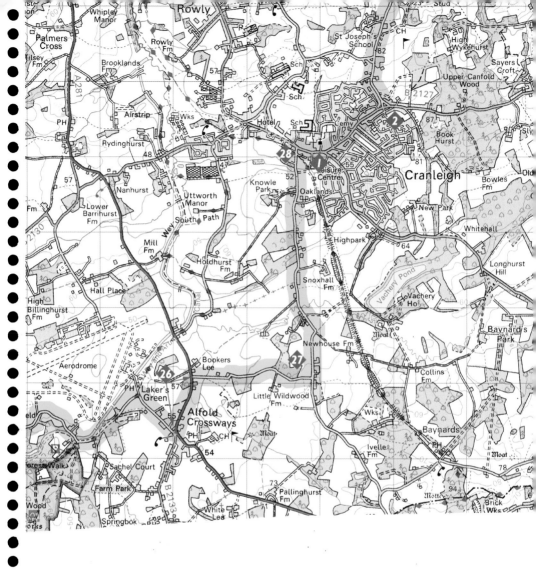

**24** After 1½ km (1 mile) 1st L on High Street Green 'Dunsfold, Cranleigh'

**25** At beginning of Dunsfold, opposite The Sun PH by memorial cross R onto Alfold Road 'Alfold, Horsham'

**26** Follow signs for Alfold and Horsham. At T-j with A281 L 'Guildford', then 1st R **take care** onto Wildwood Lane 'Cranleigh 2, Ewhurst 4'

**27** At T-j at the end of Wildwood Lane L 'Cranleigh'.

**28** At T-j in Cranleigh R to return to starting point

**3** Steep then even steeper climb through lovely woodland. At T-j R 'Ewhurst, Cranleigh', then after 400 m (yd) 1st L 'Peaslake'

**4** During the long descent, after 2½ km (1½ miles) 1st L on Lawbrook Lane by large yellow grit bin

**5** At T-j at the end of Lawbrook Lane L, then R on Burrows Lane 'Gomshall, Dorking'

**6** Follow signs for Dorking down into Gomshall. At T-j with A25 L 'Shere, Guildford'

**7** 2nd L 'Shere ¼, Ewhurst 5½, Cranleigh 7½'

**8** In Shere 1st L onto Middle Street 'Ewhurst, Cranleigh'

**9** Climb steadily for 1 km (¾ mile). Just before crossing red-brick bridge over railway, at small triangle of grass R 'Farley Green, Albury'

**10** By large triangle of grass 1st L onto Little London 'Farley Green, Shamley Green'

**11** At T-j with Brook Hill L 'Farley Green, Shamley Green'

**12** After 3 km (2 miles), having gone up and over hill, shortly after passing Madgehole Lane (no through road) on your left next L by pond onto Stroud Lane 'Cranleigh. Unsuitable for HGV'

**13** At end of Stroud Lane, at T-j with B2128 R 'Shamley Green, Guildford', then L on Upper House Lane

**14** At T-j by triangle of grass with large red-brick house ahead R (NS)

**15** At T-j with A281 R 'Bramley 1, Guildford 5' (use pavement if the road is very busy). **Easy to miss** 1st L just before sign for Birtley Green, onto public bridleway 'Private Road, Brookwell'

**16** Bear R past black iron gates. At T-J by small red-brick corner cottage with pond ahead turn L

**17** At end of Gate Street R 'Thorncombe St 1¾, Godalming 4¾'

**18** **Easy to miss** After 2½ km (1½ miles), just after beautiful half-timbered, honey-coloured house L 'Arboretum, Hascombe'

**19** At T-j with B2130 L 'Hascombe, Dunsfold', then 1st R on Mare Lane '6ft 6ins width limit' (or SA for the White Horse PH)

← two pages

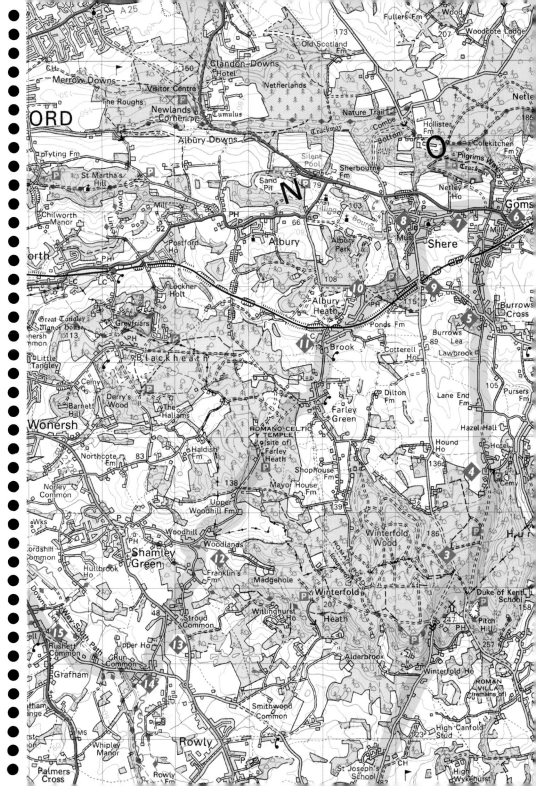

# Quiet lanes, woodland and Leith Hill, east from Cranleigh

A ride of two contrasting sections: the first half is flatter, more open and devoted to farmland; the second half climbs steeply into woodland with the opportunity of going to the very top of Leith Hill for magnificent views over the surrounding countryside. Some of the quieter lanes, such as those between Oakwoodhill and Ockley Station, are the truly perfect cycling environment. By contrast, there is one difficult junction off the A29 towards Leith Hill. Please read instruction 11 carefully.

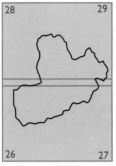

### Start

Stocklund Square, at the clock and fountain, Cranleigh

P Follow signs

### Distance and grade

45 km (28 miles)

Moderate

### Terrain

Flat or undulating as far as Capel, then a major climb of 167 m (550 ft) to Leith Hill. The road from Peaslake to Ewhurst takes the easiest line, avoiding a big climb

### Nearest railway

Ockley, or Gomshall, 3 km (2 miles) from northwest tip of route

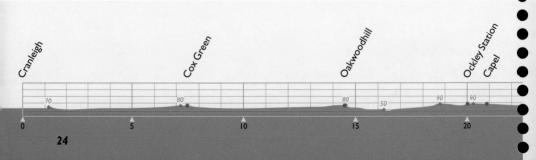

Cranleigh    Cox Green    Oakwoodhill    Ockley Station   Capel

70    80    80   50    90   90

0    5    10    15    20

## Places of interest

### Leith Hill Tower 12-13

Built in the 18th century, this tower marks the highest point in southeast England and there are wonderful views over the downs. The rhododendron wood is also worth visiting.

### Friday Street 14

Slightly off the route and approached through beautiful woodland is the hamlet of Friday Street. Comprising a lake, a few cottages and an inn, it is subject to a preservation order that helps it to retain its remoteness and tranquility. The Evelyn family (descendants of John Evelyn) are Lords of the Manor and own many of the cottages as homes for those working on the estate.

## Refreshments

*Lots of choice in* **Cranleigh**
*Thurlow Arms PH,* **Baynards**
*Punchbowl PH* 🍴🍴, **Oakwoodhill**
*Crown Inn,* **Capel**
*The Plough PH* 🍴🍴, **Coldharbour**
*Abinger Hatch* 🍴, **Abinger Common** *Volunteer Inn* 🍴, **Sutton Abinger** *Hurtwood Inn,* **Peaslake**
*Bulls Head PH* 🍴, **Ewhurst**

### Abinger Common 16

Possibly the oldest village in England, a Mesolithic Pit Dwelling dating from 5000-4000 BC was unearthed here and is the oldest preserved, man-made dwelling in the country. Nearby is the church, which was bombed during the Second World War leaving only the 13th-century chapel intact; the stocks still stand on the green in the front. There are many literary connections: the manor house was built by the 17th-century diarist John Evelyn, Sir Max Beerbohm lived at Manor Cottage and E M Forster wrote a collection of essays entitled `Abinger Harvest'.

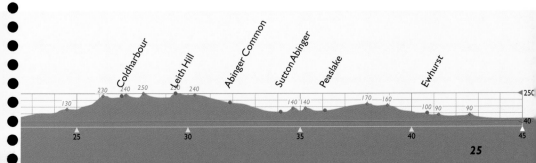

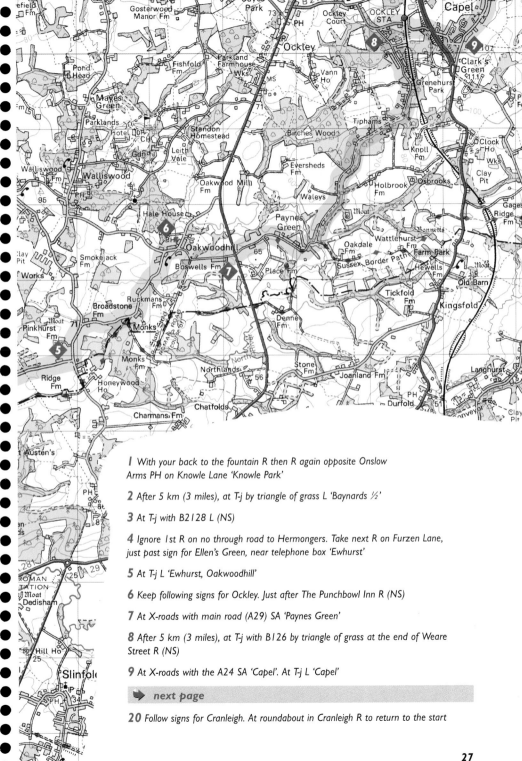

**1** With your back to the fountain R then R again opposite Onslow Arms PH on Knowle Lane 'Knowle Park'

**2** After 5 km (3 miles), at T-j by triangle of grass L 'Baynards ½'

**3** At T-j with B2128 L (NS)

**4** Ignore 1st R on no through road to Hermongers. Take next R on Furzen Lane, just past sign for Ellen's Green, near telephone box 'Ewhurst'

**5** At T-j L 'Ewhurst, Oakwoodhill'

**6** Keep following signs for Ockley. Just after The Punchbowl Inn R (NS)

**7** At X-roads with main road (A29) SA 'Paynes Green'

**8** After 5 km (3 miles), at T-j with B126 by triangle of grass at the end of Weare Street R (NS)

**9** At X-roads with the A24 SA 'Capel'. At T-j L 'Capel'

➡ **next page**

**20** Follow signs for Cranleigh. At roundabout in Cranleigh R to return to the start

**9** At X-roads with the A24 SA 'Capel'. At T-j L 'Capel'

**10** 1½ km (1 mile) after the end of Capel village on a sharp RH bend with chevrons L 'Rugge Farm'. At X-roads with A24 SA (NS)

**11** **Read carefully, dangerous right turn on blind bend.** At T-j with A29 L, then after 800 m (½ mile) 1st R. **Take extreme care: go past turning, cross road when your view is clear and return to junction**

**12** Steep climb. At T-j by triangle of grass L 'Coldharbour, Leith Hill'

**13** Go past pub and church following signs for Leith Hill. At T-j R (NS)

**14** After 3 km (2 miles) ignore 1st L to Holmbury St Mary, take next L 'Abinger Hammer'

**15** Ignore left turn onto housing estate. Take next L after 800 m (½ mile) 'Abinger Hammer'

**16** At T-j by The Volunteer PH L, then at T-j with B2126 R 'Abinger Hammer, Gomshall 1¾', then 1st L on Hoe Lane by letter box

**17** At T-j at the end of Hoe Lane L. At next T-j, L into Peaslake.

**18** After 3½ km (2¼ miles) at T-j L 'Ewhurst ¾, Cranleigh 2½'

**19** At T-j with the B2127 in Ewhurst by the Bulls Head PH R (in effect SA) 'Cranleigh 2, Guildford 12'

◀ *previous page*

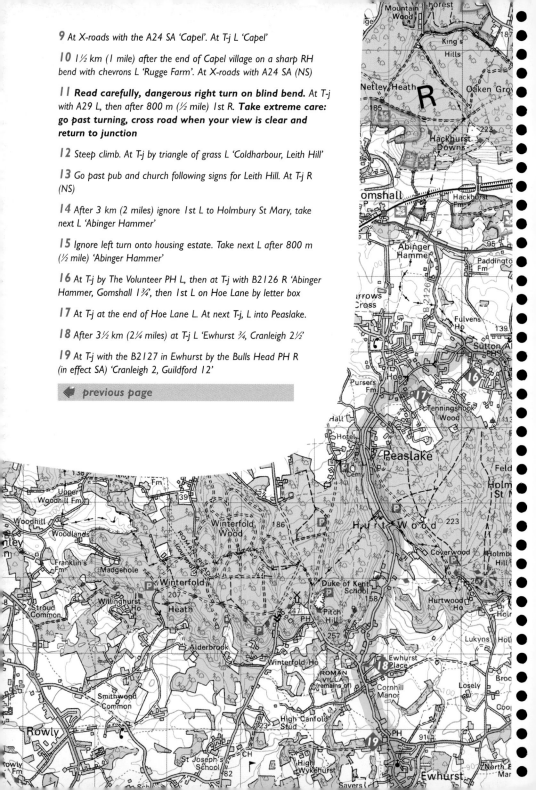

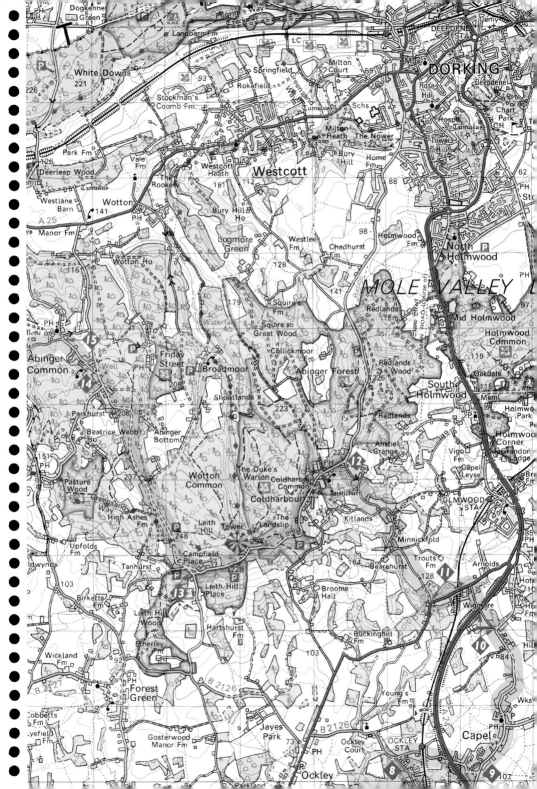

# From Edenbridge via the North Downs to Lingfield

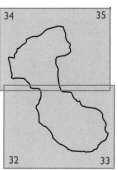

34    35

32    33

**T**he route leaves the valley formed by Eden Brook to climb through woodland skirting Oxted. Crossing first the A25, then the M25, you climb onto the North Downs and follow the ridge westwards. Dropping down to Godstone, the route continues southwards to Lingfield. Race against the horses and leave them in your wake as you enter the lovely network of lanes southeast from Dormansland. The route passes close to Hever Castle, childhood home of Anne Boleyn.

## Start

White Horse PH, High Street, Edenbridge

**P** Follow signs

## Distance and grade

53 km (33 miles)

Moderate

## Terrain

Three major climbs: 122 m (400 ft) from Edenbridge to Limpsfield Chart, 137 m (450 ft) from the A25 to Botley Hill and 100 m (330 ft) from Lingfield to southeast of Dormansland

## Nearest railway

Edenbridge

## Refreshments

Plenty of choice, **Edenbridge**
Plenty of choice, **Godstone**
Fox and Hounds, **south of Godstone**
Brickmakers Arms, **Crowhurst Lane End**
Hare and Hounds ●, **north of Lingfield**
Star PH, Old Cage PH ●, **Lingfield**
Fountain PH ●, Crown PH, **Cowden**
Kentish Horse PH, Greyhound PH, **Markbeech**

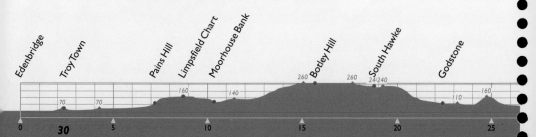

### Haxted Watermill and Museum 2
Slightly off the route, this watermill was built in 1580 and has been restored to working order.

### Detillens, Limpsfield 5
A Georgian front conceals a 15th-century timbered house. There is a Tudor morning room and a Jacobean staircase and the original central truss can still be seen in the main bedroom. An interesting collection of guns, decorations and orders is on display.

▲ *Hever Castle*

### Squerryes Court 7
Built in 1681, this William and Mary manor house contains an interesting collection of English paintings, porcelain, tapestries and furniture from the 18th century and some important Dutch old masters. The gardens have been landscaped and include a lake, formal gardens, woodland walks and an original 18th-century dovecote.

### Bletchingley 14
Slightly off the route, this pretty village is full of attractive period cottages, notably Nicholas Wolmer's, which dates back to 1552. The Whyte Hart Inn, probably the oldest building, was built in 1388. The church contains some interesting monuments.

### Hever Castle 26-27
Most famous as the childhood home of Anne Boleyn, this castle dates back to 1270 when the Gatehouse, outer walls and moat were built. In the 15th century, the Boleyn family added a Tudor home within the walls. The Astors acquired the estate in the early 20th century and restored the castle and the gardens as well as building a mock Tudor village. The house is full of the fine pictures and furniture that they collected.

Crowhurst  Lingfield  Dormansland  Cowden  Markbeech

260

70  60  130  140  80  70  70  90  130

40

30  35  40  45  50  53

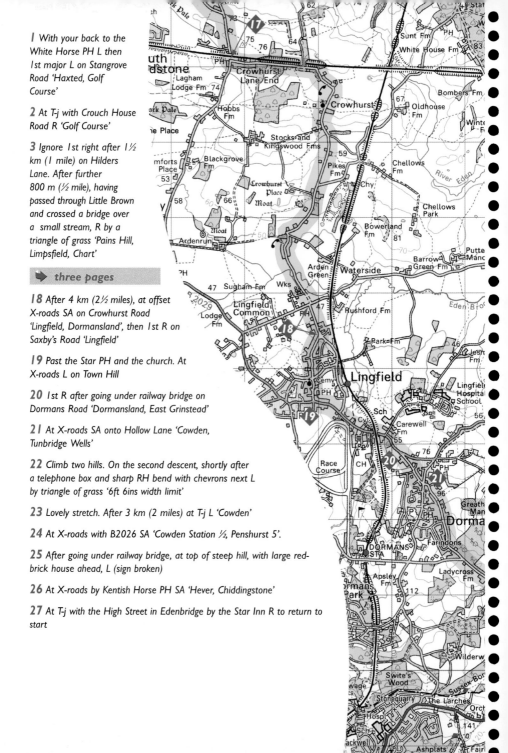

**1** With your back to the White Horse PH L then 1st major L on Stangrove Road 'Haxted, Golf Course'

**2** At T-j with Crouch House Road R 'Golf Course'

**3** Ignore 1st right after 1½ km (1 mile) on Hilders Lane. After further 800 m (½ mile), having passed through Little Brown and crossed a bridge over a small stream, R by a triangle of grass 'Pains Hill, Limpsfield, Chart'

➡ **three pages**

**18** After 4 km (2½ miles), at offset X-roads SA on Crowhurst Road 'Lingfield, Dormansland', then 1st R on Saxby's Road 'Lingfield'

**19** Past the Star PH and the church. At X-roads L on Town Hill

**20** 1st R after going under railway bridge on Dormans Road 'Dormansland, East Grinstead'

**21** At X-roads SA onto Hollow Lane 'Cowden, Tunbridge Wells'

**22** Climb two hills. On the second descent, shortly after a telephone box and sharp RH bend with chevrons next L by triangle of grass '6ft 6ins width limit'

**23** Lovely stretch. After 3 km (2 miles) at T-j L 'Cowden'

**24** At X-roads with B2026 SA 'Cowden Station ½, Penshurst 5'.

**25** After going under railway bridge, at top of steep hill, with large red-brick house ahead, L (sign broken)

**26** At X-roads by Kentish Horse PH SA 'Hever, Chiddingstone'

**27** At T-j with the High Street in Edenbridge by the Star Inn R to return to start

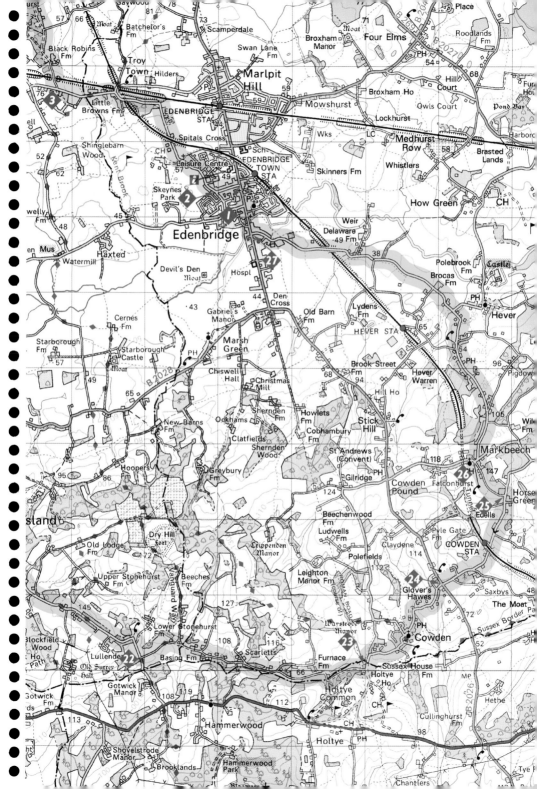

**4** *Lovely wooded section. Follow signs for Pains Hill. After 3 km (2 miles), steep climb. At brow by triangle of grass and a letter box set in a brick pillar R (NS)*

**5** *At T-j with B269 R, then L on Ridlands Lane*

**6** *At T-j by National Trust sign for Limpsfield Common L downhill*

**7** *At T-j with A25 by Grasshopper PH R, then L on Clacket Lane*

**8** *Cross M25. At T-j L then R (NS)*

**9** *At T-j with B2024 L (NS)*

**10** *At T-j with B269 R, then L on The Ridge 'Woldingham 2½'*

**11** *After 2½ km (1½ miles), on sharp RH bend with chevrons by the golf course L on Gangers Hill*

**12** *At T-j with A25 R, then at roundabout L 'Godstone'*

**13** *At the bottom of the main street bear L (in effect SA) 'Godstone Farm'*

**14** *Shortly after the Bell PH R on Tilburstow Hill 'Tilburstow Hill I'*

**15** *Climb and descend hill. Just after Fox and Hounds PH L 'South Godstone, Tandridge'*

**16** *At X-roads with A22 SA onto Miles Lane 'Tandridge, Crowhurst'*

**17** *Following signs for Crowhurst, at T-j with Tandridge Lane R 'Crowhurst, Lingfield' then 1st L immediately after railway bridge by the Brickmakers Arms onto Crowhurst Lane End 'Crowhurst'*

◀ **three pages**

# East of Edenbridge

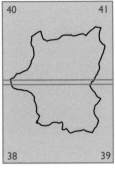

**E**scape into the countryside on this ride that passes close to both Tunbridge Wells and Sevenoaks, but takes you along tiny lanes made for cycling. After passing through the delights of Speldhurst and Leigh, you are soon faced with the demanding 183 m (600 ft) hill, with one particularly steep section beyond Underriver. Still, it is beautiful woodland and does it really matter if you get off and push? Having gained this height, you stay on the ridge until The Chart, after which there is a fast descent to Four Elms, then a 5 km (3 mile) stretch of a fairly busy road to return to the start.

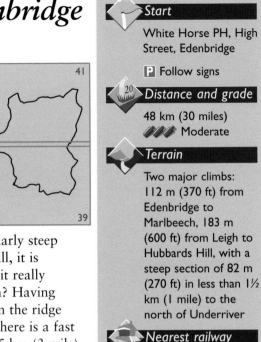

### Start

White Horse PH, High Street, Edenbridge

**P** Follow signs

### Distance and grade

48 km (30 miles)

Moderate

### Terrain

Two major climbs: 112 m (370 ft) from Edenbridge to Marlbeech, 183 m (600 ft) from Leigh to Hubbards Hill, with a steep section of 82 m (270 ft) in less than 1½ km (1 mile) to the north of Underriver

### Nearest railway

Edenbridge

### Refreshments

Plenty of choice, **Edenbridge**
Kentish Horse PH, **Markbeech**
Chafford Arms PH 🍴, **Fordcombe**
George and Dragon PH 🍴🍴, **Speldhurst**
Fleur de Lis PH, Bat and Ball PH, **Leigh**
Gate PH, **Leigh Station**
White Rock, **Underriver**
Cock Inn PH 🍴, Crown PH 🍴, **Ide Hill**

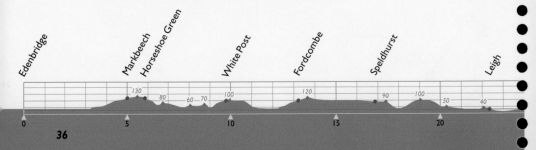

## Places of interest

### Chiddingstone village and castle 1-2
The village is owned by the National Trust and has a street
full of well-preserved 16th- and 17th-century houses. The castle
was built in 1679 and was castellated 'Gothic-style' in the early 19th century.

### Penshurst Place 11
This grand medieval manor house dates back to 1341 and was the home of the
Elizabethan poet, Sir Philip Sidney. There are formal gardens, an adventure playground
and a toy museum.

### Knole 16-17
Set around 7 courtyards and surrounded by parkland, this huge house is almost like a
village. It was built in the 15th century by Thomas Bouchier, Archbishop of Canterbury

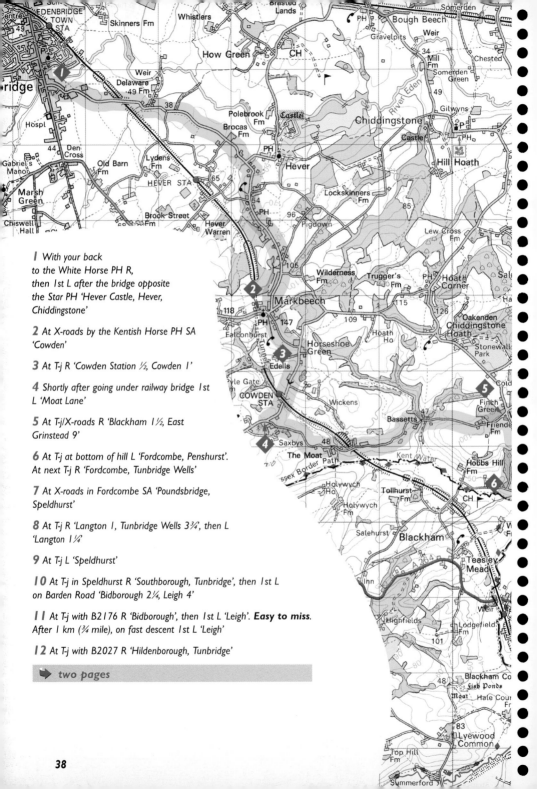

**1** With your back
to the White Horse PH R,
then 1st L after the bridge opposite
the Star PH 'Hever Castle, Hever,
Chiddingstone'

**2** At X-roads by the Kentish Horse PH SA
'Cowden'

**3** At T-j R 'Cowden Station ½, Cowden 1'

**4** Shortly after going under railway bridge 1st
L 'Moat Lane'

**5** At T-j/X-roads R 'Blackham 1½, East
Grinstead 9'

**6** At T-j at bottom of hill L 'Fordcombe, Penshurst'.
At next T-j R 'Fordcombe, Tunbridge Wells'

**7** At X-roads in Fordcombe SA 'Poundsbridge,
Speldhurst'

**8** At T-j R 'Langton 1, Tunbridge Wells 3¾', then L
'Langton 1¼'

**9** At T-j L 'Speldhurst'

**10** At T-j in Speldhurst R 'Southborough, Tunbridge', then 1st L
on Barden Road 'Bidborough 2¼, Leigh 4'

**11** At T-j with B2176 R 'Bidborough', then 1st L 'Leigh'. **Easy to miss.**
After 1 km (¾ mile), on fast descent 1st L 'Leigh'

**12** At T-j with B2027 R 'Hildenborough, Tunbridge'

➡ two pages

38

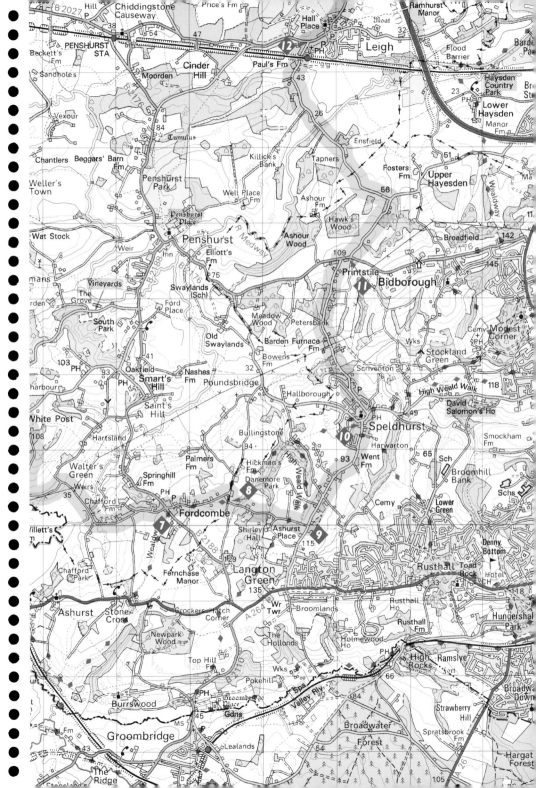

**12** At T-j with B2027 R 'Hildenborough, Tunbridge'

**13** Under the A21, then 1st L 'Sevenoaks (B245)'

**14** After 1 km (¾ mile), at T-j with B245 L 'Sevenoaks', then R on Mill Lane

**15** Follow signs for Underriver. Steep hill. As it levels 1st L on Fawke Wood Road 'River Hill 1½, Sevenoaks 3'

**16** At T-j L 'Sevenoaks'

**17** At T-j with A225 R, then 1st L on Gracious Lane 'Ide Hill 3'

**18** At X-roads with Weald Road SA on continuation of Gracious Lane

**19** After 1½ km (1 mile), as road runs parallel with sunken A21 L on bridge over main road, then 1st R 'Ide Hill 2¼, Edenbridge 7'

**20** At T-j with B2042 L (NS), then 1st R after sharp RH bend 'Ide Hill ¼, Sundridge 1½'

**21** In Ide Hill follow roundabout to R, then 1st L immediately after National Trust Property Emmetts Garden

**22** At T-j L 'Toys Hill ½, Four Elms 2½, Edenbridge 5'.

**23** At T-j with B2042 on sharp bend R (in effect SA) 'Four Elms ½, Edenbridge 3'. Busy stretch. At T-j in Edenbridge L to return to start

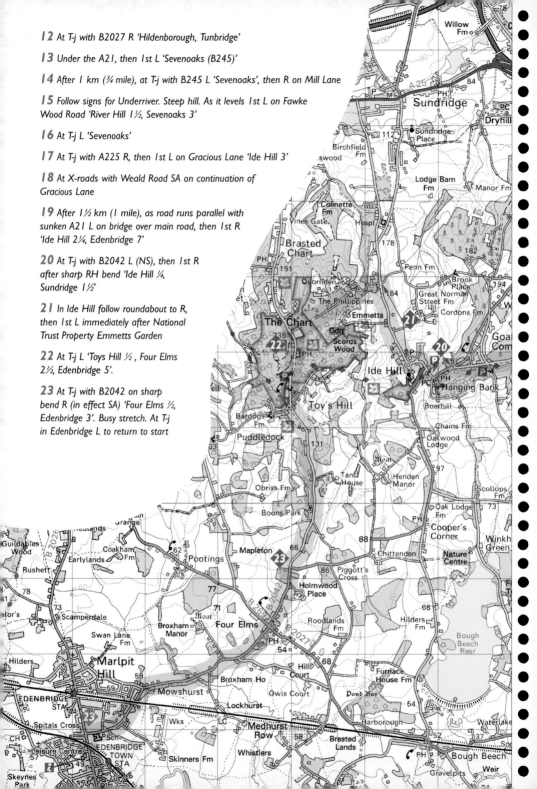

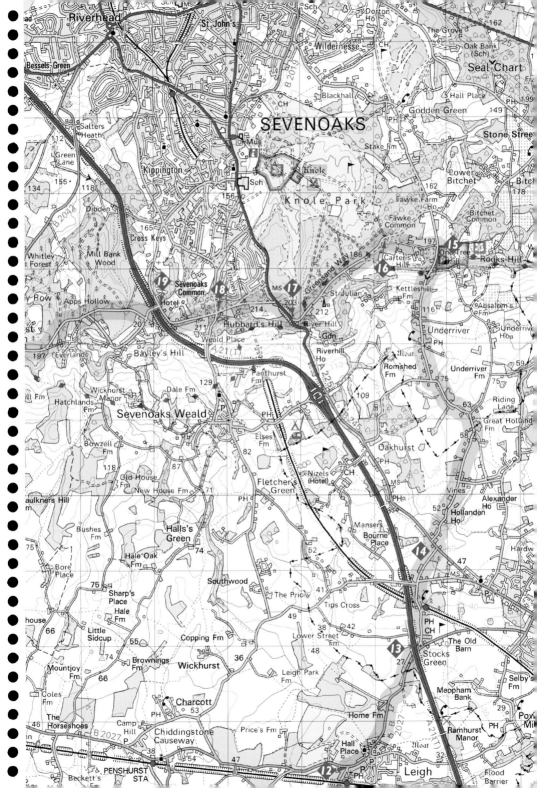

# 7 East from Headcorn up onto the North Downs

The North Downs offer some of the best road rides in the southeast with a maze of quiet lanes, some steep challenges and panoramic views down into the Weald. Although very much like the West Country, the occasional appearance of oast houses, fruit orchards and hop plantations remind you that this is Kent, the garden of England. The ride climbs north from Headcorn, passing the estate of Leeds Castle, crossing the M20 to Hollingbourne before the steepest climb of the day up onto the escarpment of the North Downs at Hucking. Several short climbs and descents through woodland and past fruit orchards drop you down at Doddington before the second major climb up onto the top of the North Downs above Charing Heath. Beyond Pembles Cross, the ride is mostly flat back to Headcorn.

### Start

The George & Dragon PH, the High Street, Headcorn, southeast of Maidstone

P Signposted car park just off the main street

### Distance and grade

51 km (32 miles)

Strenuous

### Terrain

The North Downs have many unexpected climbs! Steady 122 m (400 ft) climb from Headcorn to Kingswood. Steep 82 m (270 ft) climb from Broad Street to Hucking. Steady 122 m (400 ft) climb south from Doddington to the high point. Several more short climbs. Lowest point – 21 m (70 ft) at the start. Highest point – 195 m (640 ft) at the top of the North Downs before the descent to Charing Heath

### Nearest railway

Headcorn

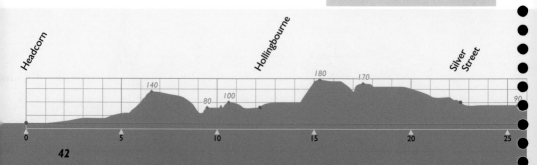

## Places of interest

### Headcorn 1

Until 1815, when French prisoners of war completed the present main road, the road between Tenterden and Maidstone ran straight past the church, instead of diverting northwards as it does today. Church Walk, a string of cottages leading towards the church, was once a continuation of the High Street. An avenue of chestnuts, planted to commemorate Queen Victoria's Diamond Jubilee, flanks the other side of the churchyard. At the end, an ancient oak stands by the church – a lonely survivor of the days when Headcorn was a clearing in the great Wealden Forest. Headcorn has rows of weatherboarded and tile-hung cottages, and several half-timbered houses

### Leeds Castle 6

Kings and modern statesmen have trodden the floors of the lake-bound castle whose history goes back 1000 years. Inside, there are rich furnishings and paintings, outside an aviary and a maze in the sublime setting of the grounds landscaped by Capability Brown

## Refreshments

Plenty of choice in **Headcorn**
(Pepper Box PH ●●, **Ulcombe**,
just off the route, instruction 3)
Dirty Habit PH ●,
**Hollingbourne**
Hook & Hatchet PH, **Hucking**
Sun PH, **Bredgar**
Chequers Inn, **Doddington**
George PH ●●, **Newnham**,
(just off the route)
Harrow PH ●, **Warren Street**
Bowl PH, southeast of
**Warren Street**
Red Lion PH, **Charing Heath**

▲ Leeds Castle

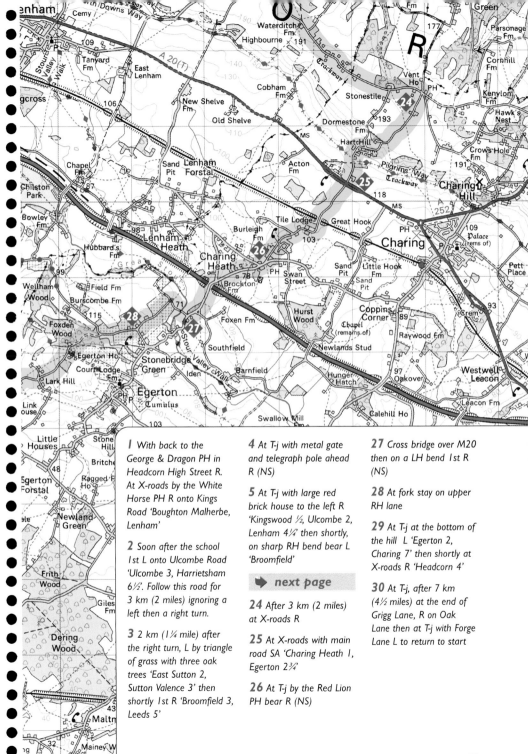

**1** With back to the George & Dragon PH in Headcorn High Street R. At X-roads by the White Horse PH R onto Kings Road 'Boughton Malherbe, Lenham'

**2** Soon after the school 1st L onto Ulcombe Road 'Ulcombe 3, Harrietsham 6½'. Follow this road for 3 km (2 miles) ignoring a left then a right turn.

**3** 2 km (1¼ mile) after the right turn, L by triangle of grass with three oak trees 'East Sutton 2, Sutton Valence 3' then shortly 1st R 'Broomfield 3, Leeds 5'

**4** At T-j with metal gate and telegraph pole ahead R (NS)

**5** At T-j with large red brick house to the left R 'Kingswood ½, Ulcombe 2, Lenham 4¼' then shortly, on sharp RH bend bear L 'Broomfield'

➡ **next page**

**24** After 3 km (2 miles) at X-roads R

**25** At X-roads with main road SA 'Charing Heath 1, Egerton 2¾'

**26** At T-j by the Red Lion PH bear R (NS)

**27** Cross bridge over M20 then on a LH bend 1st R (NS)

**28** At fork stay on upper RH lane

**29** At T-j at the bottom of the hill L 'Egerton 2, Charing 7' then shortly at X-roads R 'Headcorn 4'

**30** At T-j, after 7 km (4½ miles) at the end of Grigg Lane, R on Oak Lane then at T-j with Forge Lane L to return to start

**45**

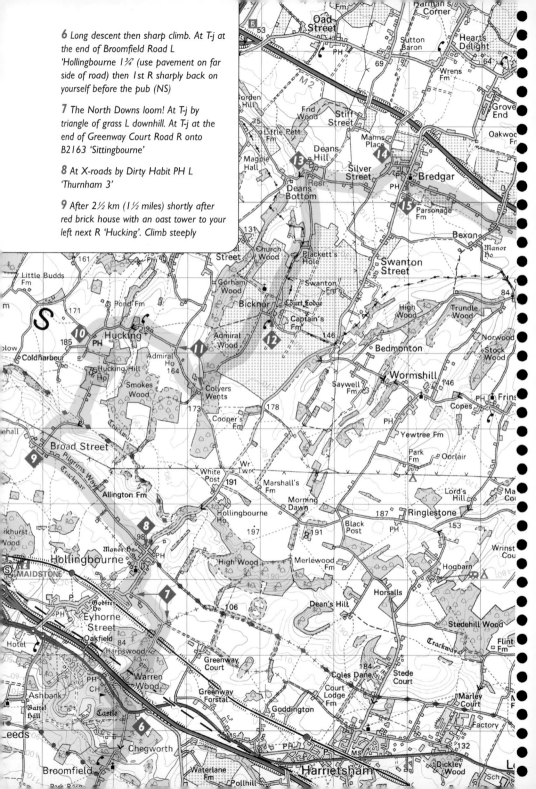

**6** Long descent then sharp climb. At T-j at the end of Broomfield Road L 'Hollingbourne 1¾ (use pavement on far side of road) then 1st R sharply back on yourself before the pub (NS)

**7** The North Downs loom! At T-j by triangle of grass L downhill. At T-j at the end of Greenway Court Road R onto B2163 'Sittingbourne'

**8** At X-roads by Dirty Habit PH L 'Thurnham 3'

**9** After 2½ km (1½ miles) shortly after red brick house with an oast tower to your left next R 'Hucking'. Climb steeply

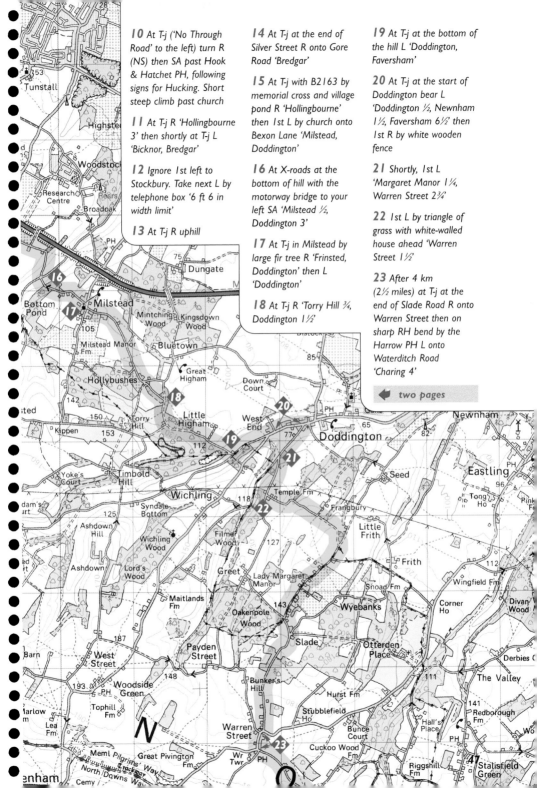

**10** At T-j ('No Through Road' to the left) turn R (NS) then SA past Hook & Hatchet PH, following signs for Hucking. Short steep climb past church

**11** At T-j R 'Hollingbourne 3' then shortly at T-j L 'Bicknor, Bredgar'

**12** Ignore 1st left to Stockbury. Take next L by telephone box '6 ft 6 in width limit'

**13** At T-j R uphill

**14** At T-j at the end of Silver Street R onto Gore Road 'Bredgar'

**15** At T-j with B2163 by memorial cross and village pond R 'Hollingbourne' then 1st L by church onto Bexon Lane 'Milstead, Doddington'

**16** At X-roads at the bottom of hill with the motorway bridge to your left SA 'Milstead ½, Doddington 3'

**17** At T-j in Milstead by large fir tree R 'Frinsted, Doddington' then L 'Doddington'

**18** At T-j R 'Torry Hill ¾, Doddington 1½'

**19** At T-j at the bottom of the hill L 'Doddington, Faversham'

**20** At T-j at the start of Doddington bear L 'Doddington ½, Newnham 1½, Faversham 6½' then 1st R by white wooden fence

**21** Shortly, 1st L 'Margaret Manor 1¼, Warren Street 2¾'

**22** 1st L by triangle of grass with white-walled house ahead 'Warren Street 1½'

**23** After 4 km (2½ miles) at T-j at the end of Slade Road R onto Warren Street then on sharp RH bend by the Harrow PH L onto Waterditch Road 'Charing 4'

← two pages

47

# 8 West from Headcorn through the orchards of Kent

A look at the map of the area shows to what extent the agriculture of the region is dominated by fruit orchards. This ride runs along quiet lanes through the flat area formed by the tributaries of the River Medway, the Beult and the Teise, passing many oast houses and fruit orchards, which are a real delight when in full blossom from mid-April to the end of May.

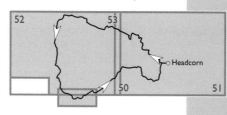

 **Start**

George & Dragon PH, High Street, Headcorn, southeast of Maidstone

P Parking signposted off the Main Street

 **Distance and grade**

46 km (29 miles)

Easy

**Terrain**

A flat ride with two small climbs, one either side of Horsmonden. Lowest point – 10 m (35 ft) at the crossing of the River Medway near Yalding. Highest point – 73 m (240 ft) at Winchet Hill, east of Horsmonden

 **Nearest railway**

Headcorn

**Refreshments**

Plenty of choice in **Headcorn**
Walnut Tree PH 🍴, Two Brewers PH,
George PH, **Yalding**
Chequers PH, **Laddingford**
Kent Arms PH, south of **Laddingford**
Castle Inn, **Castle Hill**
Gun & Spitroast PH 🍴,
Highwayman PH, **Horsmonden**
Lord Raglan PH 🍴, **Staplehurst**

**Boughton Monchelsea Place** 6/7 *(just off the route)*
Battlemented Elizabethan manor house of cool grey
Kentish ragstone. Superb views across the deer park to the
hazy expanse of the Weald.
Tudor kitchens and displays of
carriages and farm implements

### Yalding 10
Two long, stone, medieval
bridges lead into the wide
curving street of mellow brick
and timber houses. The Teise
and Beult rivers flow into the
Medway in the heart of Kent's
hop-farming country. Warde's
Moat is a picturesque vicarage
encircled by water

### Horsmonden 18
Orchards and hop gardens sur-
round an assortment of Kentish
houses around the village green.
At Gun Inn, John Browne made
guns for Charles I, Cromwell,
the British Navy and the Dutch.
The dark water of the furnace
pond are a relic of the Wealden
iron industry. Sprivers Gardens,
set in a 44 ha (108 acre) park

▲ *Yalding Church*

surrounding an 18th-century mansion, contain rare plants,
temples and a garden statuary

### Iden Croft Herbs 24 *(south of the route)*
Famous herb gardens fill the air with a heady fragrance.
There are culinary, medicinal, aromatic and decorative
herbs for sale

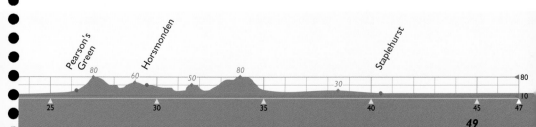

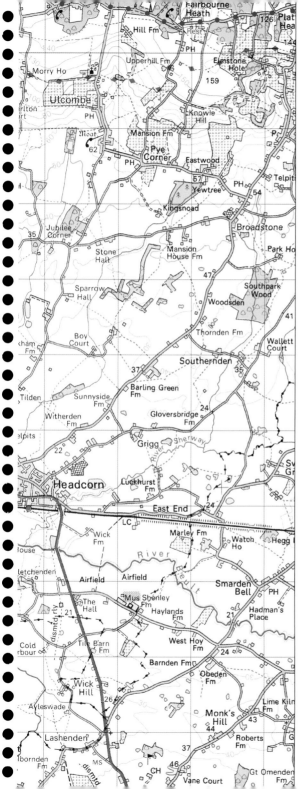

**1** With back to the George & Dragon PH, R. After 400 m (yd), immediately after White Horse PH, L onto Moat Road 'Frittenden, Staplehurst'

**2** At T-j after 3 km (2 miles) R 'Sutton Valence, Maidstone'

**3** After 800 m (½ mile) 1st L onto Babylon Lane 'Chart Sutton'

**4** Easy to miss. After 3 km (2 miles) 1st L by triangle of grass, cypress trees and red brick house with wooden fence (NS)

**5** At T-j with tall wooden gate/fence ahead L (NS)

**6** Ignore 1st right to Boughton Monchelsea. Take 2nd R on Lower Farm Road 'Rabbits Cross'

➡ **next page**

**23** At T-j with Pagehurst Road R 'Staplehurst 1, Headcorn 5'

**24** At X-roads with Station Road (A229) SA onto Headorn Road 'Hawkenbury, Headcorn'

**25** After 1 km (¾ mile) 1st proper R onto Cradduck Lane 'Frittenden 2½'

**26** At T-j L 'Frittenden 1½'

**27** At T-j L 'Headcorn 2½, Lenham 9'

**28** At T-j R 'Headcorn ¼, Lenham 7'

**29** At X-roads with A274 in Headcorn R onto North Street 'Biddenden, Tenterden' to return to start

**7** Ignore right and left turns for 4 km (2½ miles). At T-j with A229 at the end of Butt Green Lane R then 1st L on Redwall Lane 'Hunton, Yalding'

**8** At T-j at the end of Redwall Lane R 'Hunton, Yalding, Maidstone'

**9** At offset X-roads L then R onto Lughorse Lane 'Farleigh Green 1¾, West Farleigh 2½'

**10** At T-j at the end of Lughorse Lane L 'Yalding ¼, East Peckham 3 ½, Horsmonden 7'

**11** Cross bridge. At T-j with B2162 R 'East Peckham 3, Paddock Wood 4, Tonbridge 8½'

**12** After 400 m (¼ mile) 1st L onto Lees Road 'Laddingford, Paddock Wood 3¾'

**13** Shortly after Chequers PH R onto Darman Lane 'Brenchley 4, Paddock Wood 3'

**14** Ignore 1st L by Kent Arms PH. Take next L on Willow Lane 'Brenchley, Horsemonden'

**15** At T-j with Pearson's Green Road bear L (NS)

**16** On sharp LH bend R 'Castle Hill, Horsmonden'

**17** At T-j by Castle Inn at the end of Pearson's Green Road L 'Horsmonden 1½' then 1st R onto Furnace Lane 'Horsmonden 1¼'

**18** At T-j at the end of Furnace Lane L following signs for Goudhurst and Cranbrook

**19** At T-j with B2079 by triangle of grass L 'Marden 4, Maidstone 12'

**20** Past orchard. 800 m (½ mile) after passing beneath power lines at top of hill R 'Curtisden Green ¼'

**21** Through Curtisden Green. After 2 km (1¼ mile) ignore right to Colliers Green. Shortly, take the next R 'Staplehurst 2½'

**22** After 1 km (¾ mile) 1st L 'Marden Thorn'

**23** At T-j with Pagehurst Road R 'Staplehurst 1, Headcorn 5'

◀ previous page

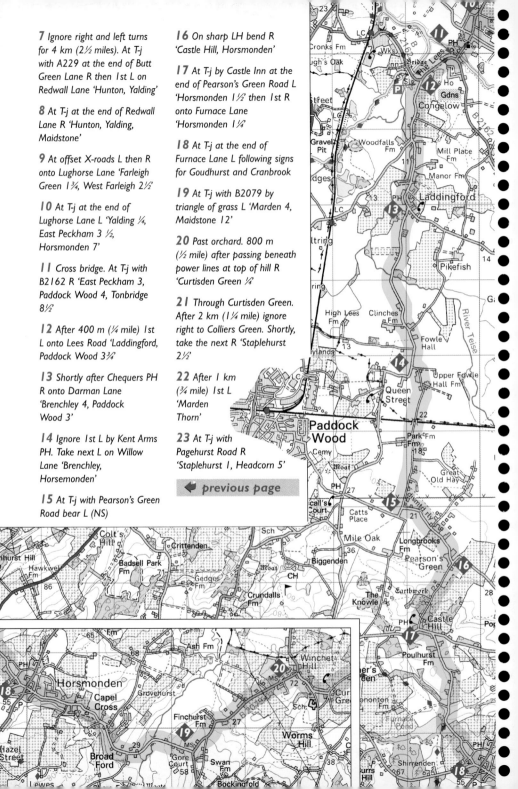

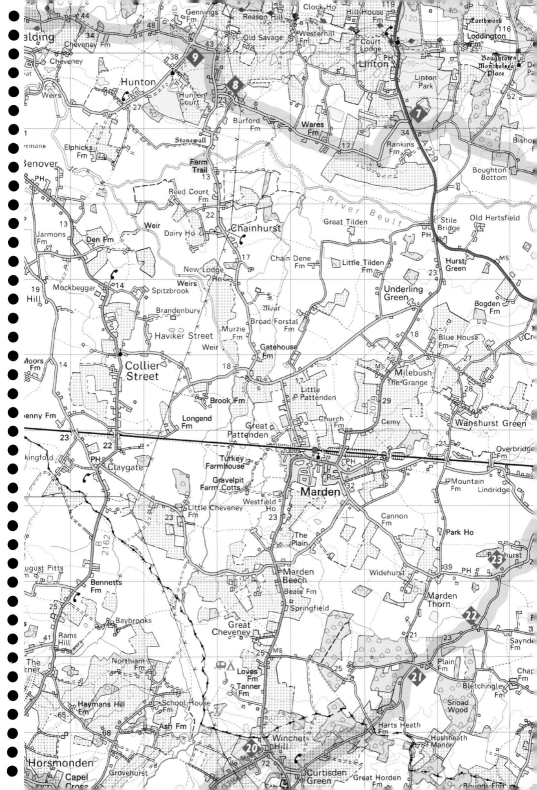

# West from Cranbrook through the Weald of Kent and Sussex

The Weald lies betwen the North and South Downs and in the main consists of thick clay soil that is the bane of off-road riding – the off-road circuit of Bewl Water is almost impassable in the winter months. However, there are some delightful lanes throughout the area and with careful planning it is possible to avoid the main roads for all but the shortest link sections. The heavy clay soil is the ideal growing environment for broad leaf woodland and there are many fragments left of what was once a huge forest almost entirely covering the Weald, which went by the evocative name of Anderida.

| 59 | 60 |
| 56 |
| Cranbrook |
| 57 | 58 |

## Start

George Hotel, High Street, Cranbrook, 19 km (12 miles) south of Maidstone on the A229

P Large car park near to the supermarket in the centre of Cranbrook

## Distance and grade

53 km (33 miles)

Moderate

## Terrain

Lowest point – 15 m (50 ft) at the crossing of the tributaries of the River Rother east of Hurst Green. Highest point – 170 m (560 ft) at Sparrows Green near Wadhurst

## Nearest railway

Wadhurst Station, 2 km (1¼ mile) west of Wadhurst

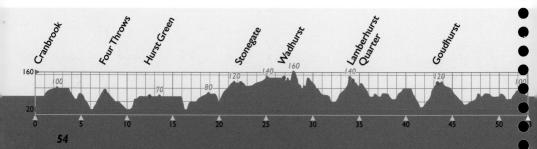

Cranbrook · Four Throws · Hurst Green · Stonegate · Wadhurst · Lamberhurst Quarter · Goudhurst

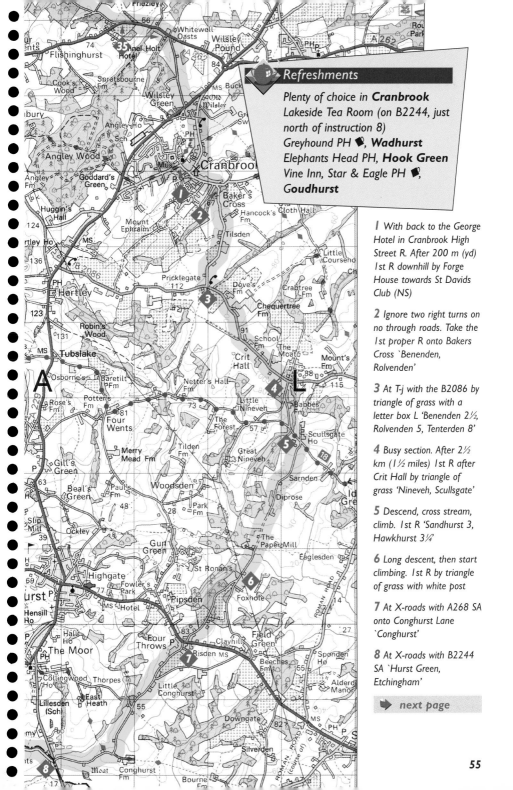

➡️ next page

**Refreshments**

Plenty of choice in **Cranbrook**
Lakeside Tea Room (on B2244, just
north of instruction 8)
Greyhound PH 🍴, **Wadhurst**
Elephants Head PH, **Hook Green**
Vine Inn, Star & Eagle PH 🍴,
**Goudhurst**

*1* With back to the George
Hotel in Cranbrook High
Street R. After 200 m (yd)
1st R downhill by Forge
House towards St Davids
Club (NS)

*2* Ignore two right turns on
no through roads. Take the
1st proper R onto Bakers
Cross `Benenden,
Rolvenden'

*3* At T-j with the B2086 by
triangle of grass with a
letter box L 'Benenden 2½,
Rolvenden 5, Tenterden 8'

*4* Busy section. After 2½
km (1½ miles) 1st R after
Crit Hall by triangle of
grass 'Nineveh, Scullsgate'

*5* Descend, cross stream,
climb. 1st R 'Sandhurst 3,
Hawkhurst 3¼'

*6* Long descent, then start
climbing. 1st R by triangle
of grass with white post

*7* At X-roads with A268 SA
onto Conghurst Lane
`Conghurst'

*8* At X-roads with B2244
SA `Hurst Green,
Etchingham'

**8** At X-roads with B2244 SA 'Hurst Green, Etchingham'

**9** At T-j with A229 L 'Battle 8, Hurst Green ¾'

**10** At T-j with A21 L 'Battle 8, Hurst Green ½' then 1st R onto Station Road 'A265 Lewes, Etchingham Station 2'

**11** Ignore right turns onto housing estates. At the end of the village R 'Burgh Hill'

**12** After 800 m (½ mile) shortly after brow of hill 1st R by triangle of grass and cypress trees (NS)

**13** Steep descent, steep climb. At T-j bear R (in effect SA) 'Ticehurst 3, Stonegate 3'

**14** At T-j at the end of Sheep Street by triangle of grass L 'Stonegate 1, Burwash 3'

**15** At T-j / X-roads bear R 'Wadhurst 2½'

**16** At T-j with B2099 L 'Wadhurst 1, Frant 5, Tunbridge Wells 8'

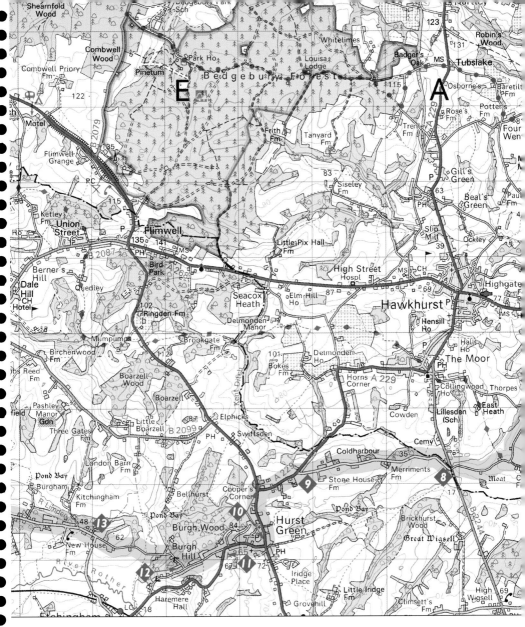

**17** After 2½ km (1½ miles) 1st (sharp) R in Wadhurst onto Blacksmiths Lane just before the bank, opposite the Greyhound PH

**18** At fork, at the bottom of the hill bear L steeply uphill

**19** At X-road SA onto Turner's Green Road. At fork bear R. At T-j bear R 'Wood's Green, Bells Yew Green'

**20** At top of climb bear R 'Hook Green, Cousley Wood'. SA at two closely spaced X-roads (Give Way) 'Hook Green 1¼'

**21** SA third X-roads (your right of way) then shortly bear L by triangle of grass 'Hook Green 1'

▶ *next page*

**20** At top of climb bear R 'Hook Green, Cousley Wood'. SA at two closely spaced X-roads (Give Way) 'Hook Green 1¼'

**21** SA third X-roads (your right of way) then shortly bear L by triangle of grass 'Hook Green 1'

**22** At X-roads at the end of Free Heath Road SA onto Clay Hill Road 'Kippings Cross 3, Pembury 4fi'

**23** At top of hill, with red tile house ahead R onto Perch Lane

**24** At T-j (with A21) at the end of Perch Lane R 'Lamberhurst 2, Goudhurst 5'. **Take care** – very busy section. After 1 km (¾ mile) 1st L onto Cuckoo Lane

**25** At T-j at the end of Cuckoo Lane L onto Tong Road then 1st R by small triangle of grass 'Horsmonden, Goudhurst'

**26** At fork at the top of the hill shortly after Ruck Farm R. At X-roads (with B2162) at the end of Ruck Lane SA 'Goudhurst 2¾'

**27** At T-j (with a laurel hedge to your left) R (NS) then 1st L 'Horsmonden Church'

**28** At X-roads by a triangle of grass SA onto Smallbridge Road

**29** Ignore 1st right to Lamberhurst. Take next R by grit bin and yellow hydrant (NS). At T-j (with B2079) at the top of the hill R

**30** At X-roads in Goudhurst L 'Cranbrook 5, Hawkhurst 6, Ashford 21'

**31** 400 m (yd) after church 1st L (NS). At X-roads with B2084 SA (NS)

**32** At T-j by letter box R (NS) (740395) then shortly 1st R 'Blantyre House'

**33** At T-j by triangle of grass R towards brick houses on the horizon

**34** At T-j at the end of Round Green Lane R onto Colliers Green Road 'Goudhurst' then shortly 1st L by letterbox (NS)

**35** At T-j with A262 L 'Sissinghurst, Cranbrook, Ashford' then 1st R by red brick arch (NS). At T-j R then L and L again. Shortly at next T-j L. At T-j at the end of Quaker Lane R downhill to return to the start

← four pages

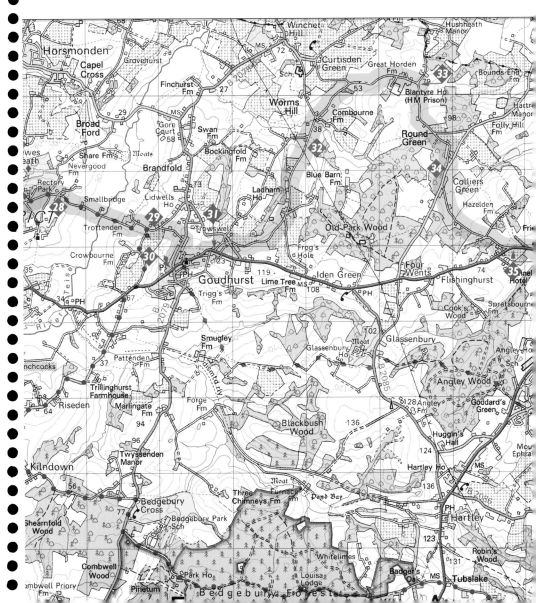

# Tenterden to Sissinghurst Castle

**A** satisfying ride that takes in points of interest such as Sissinghurst Castle and the windmill at Woodchurch, the attractive villages of Headcorn, Smarden and Pluckley, some good pubs and wonderful scenery.

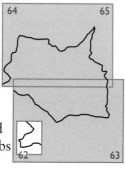

Although the road between Tenterden and Sissinghurst is at times busy, this is soon forgotten as you turn off towards the old-world beauty of Sissinghurst Castle. The bridlepath that takes you through the estate may at times be a little rough but this diversion from the main road and past such a magnificent property is fine compensation for any slight discomfort.

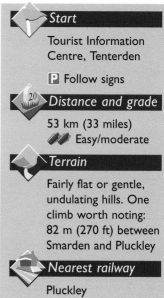

### Start

Tourist Information Centre, Tenterden

**P** Follow signs

### Distance and grade

53 km (33 miles)

Easy/moderate

### Terrain

Fairly flat or gentle, undulating hills. One climb worth noting: 82 m (270 ft) between Smarden and Pluckley

### Nearest railway

Pluckley

### Refreshments

Lots of choice in **Tenterden**
Bull Inn ♥, **Sissinghurst**
Coffee and tea at **Sissinghurst Castle**
Bell and Jorrods PH, **Frittenden**
Kings Arms PH, George and Dragon PH ♥, **Headcorn**
The Bell PH ♥♥, Smarden Bell PH, Chequers PH ♥, **Smarden**
Black Horse PH ♥, **Pluckley**
Dering Arms PH ♥♥, **Pluckley Station**
Bonny Cravat PH, Six Bells PH, **Woodchurch**

### Sissinghurst Garden 3

These gardens were created by Vita Sackville West and her husband Sir Harold Nicholson in the 1930s. A series of small gardens are enclosed within the remains of an Elizabethan mansion.

### Headcorn Flower Centre and Vineyard 7-8

Award-winning wine is produced at this vineyard and can be tasted free of charge at the end of a visit. Chrysanthemums and orchid lilies bloom all year round in the flower houses and there is a large reservoir stocked with trout.

### Smarden 10

This an old wool village with an Elizabethan market place and many interesting old buildings. The large parish church has a copy of an Elizabethan charter granting permission for a weekly market and an annual fair.

### Woodchurch Windmill 14-15

This restored smock mill, now in working order, contains an exhibition charting the mill's history.

### Rare Breeds Centre, Woodchurch 15

Ninety acres of farmland house this important collection of rare animals. There is a 'kiddies corner' where many young animals can be handled.

### Tenterden 16-17

The name Tenterden comes from the earliest settlement: a pig pasture for the men of Thanet. By the 14th century, sheep were the main source of wealth and a flourishing cloth industry developed. Tenterden prospered and became a member of the Confederation of the Cinque Ports. St Mildred's Church dominates the main street with its impressive pinnacled tower built in the 15th century of Bethersden marble. The 13th-century chancel is the oldest section of the church and has an early English lancet window with a modern stained glass representation of St Mildred. The Woolpack Inn and the Tudor Rose date from the 15th century and, unlike some other buildings in the High Street (such as the Eight Bells Inn), have not been given 18th- or 19th-century facades.

### The Tenterden and District Museum 17

This explains the town's interesting history and also houses a railway museum. The main station nearby was closed in 1954 but now runs steam train trips into the Wealden countryside.

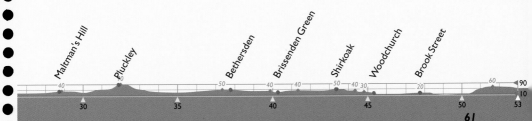

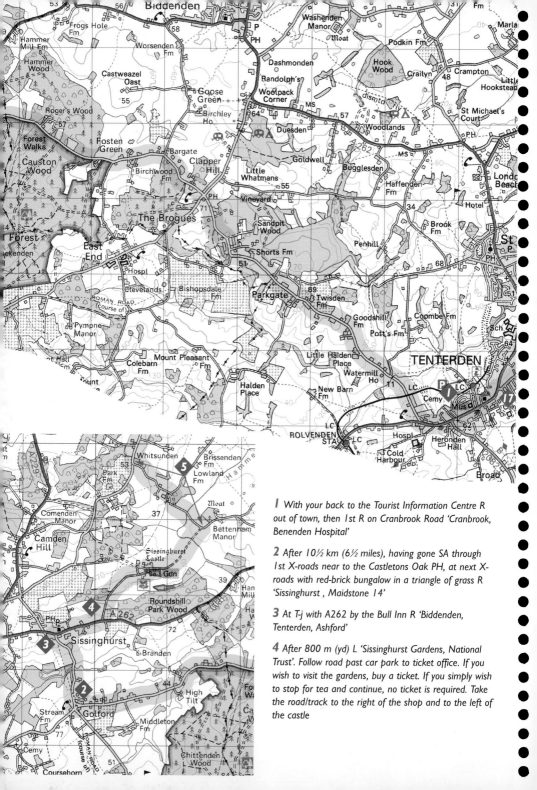

**1** With your back to the Tourist Information Centre R out of town, then 1st R on Cranbrook Road 'Cranbrook, Benenden Hospital'

**2** After 10½ km (6½ miles), having gone SA through 1st X-roads near to the Castletons Oak PH, at next X-roads with red-brick bungalow in a triangle of grass R 'Sissinghurst , Maidstone 14'

**3** At T-j with A262 by the Bull Inn R 'Biddenden, Tenterden, Ashford'

**4** After 800 m (yd) L 'Sissinghurst Gardens, National Trust'. Follow road past car park to ticket office. If you wish to visit the gardens, buy a ticket. If you simply wish to stop for tea and continue, no ticket is required. Take the road/track to the right of the shop and to the left of the castle

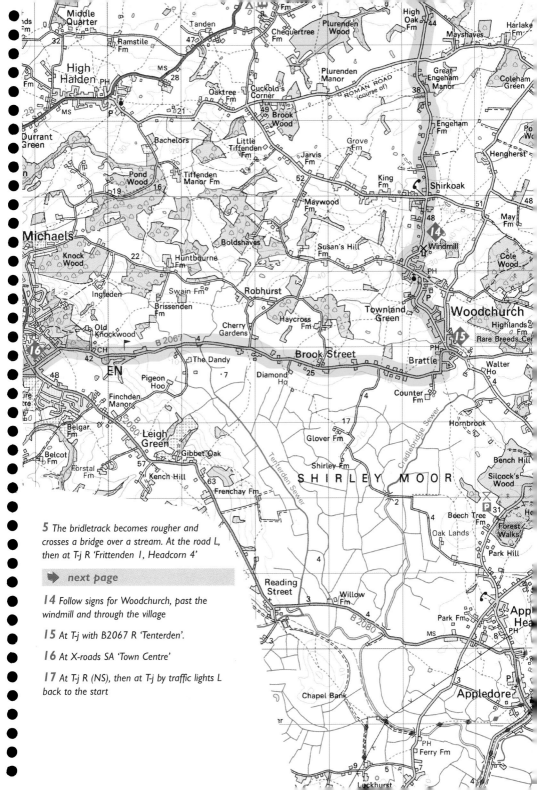

**5** The bridletrack becomes rougher and crosses a bridge over a stream. At the road L, then at T-j R 'Frittenden 1, Headcorn 4'

➡ **next page**

**14** Follow signs for Woodchurch, past the windmill and through the village

**15** At T-j with B2067 R 'Tenterden'.

**16** At X-roads SA 'Town Centre'

**17** At T-j R (NS), then at T-j by traffic lights L back to the start

**6** Through Frittenden, following signs for Headcorn. At T-j R 'Headcorn ¼, Lenham 7'

**7** At X-roads with A274 R on North Street 'Biddenden, Tenterden'

**8** On sharp RH bend at end of village L 'Smarden'

**9** At T-j by The Bell PH L 'Smarden', then 1st R 'Smarden'

**10** In Smarden at T-j by Chequers PH L

**11** After 5½ km (3½ miles), in Pluckley at top of the hill R 'Bethersden'

**12** After 5½ km (3½ miles) you will pass a timber frame works. At X-roads SA 'Great Chart, Ashford', then 1st R on Kiln Lane

**13** At T-j with A28 L (NS), then after 800 m (½ mile) 1st R ' Woodchurch 4'

◀ previous page

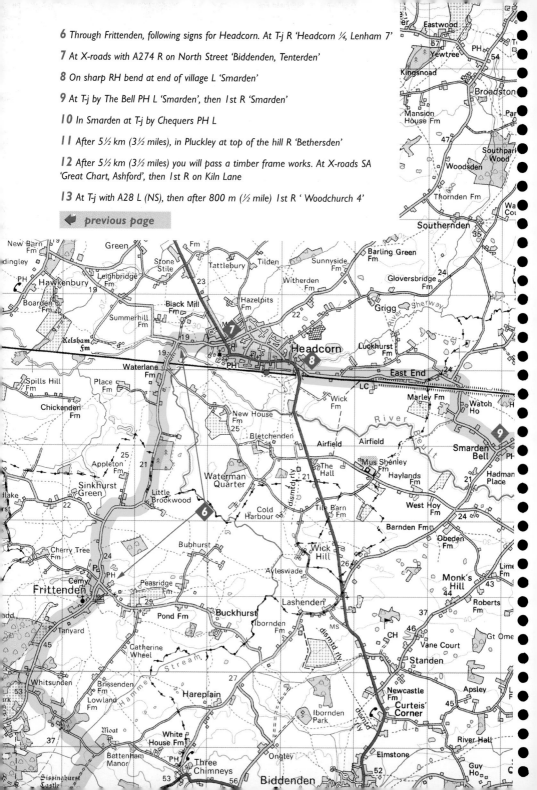

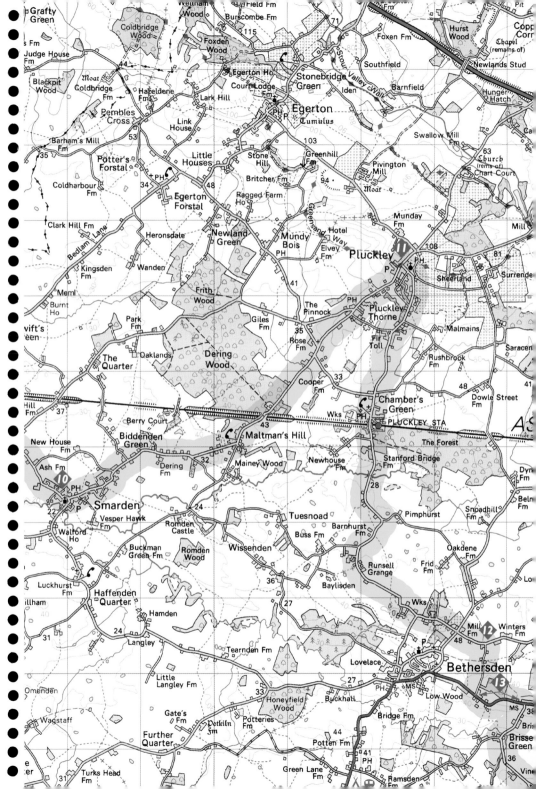

# Wye to Chilham

This ride features lots of stretches of beautiful lanes linked together in an exploration of the rolling downland between the A20/M20 and the A2/M2. The scenery is typical of Kent, with many oast houses, orchards and fields of hops. The village of Chilham is a real delight with pubs, tea shops and a castle to visit. The ride finishes with some lovely wooded lanes through Sole Street and Crundale.

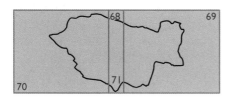

## Start

The church in Wye

P Follow signs to free parking near start

## Distance and grade

51 km (32 miles)
Moderate

## Terrain

Two climbs of 122 m (400 ft) – between Westwell and Charing Hill and between Shalmsford Street and Sole Street. Several short, steep hills, The Wynd just north of Charing is fiercesome!

## Nearest railway

Wye

## Refreshments

New Flying Horse PH 🍺, Tickled Trout PH 🍺, **Wye**
Flying Horse PH 🍺🍺, **Boughton Lees**
Wheel Inn, **Westwell**
Bowl Inn, **north of Charing Hill**
The Plough PH 🍺, **Shottenden**
White Horse PH 🍺🍺, Woolpack PH 🍺,
tea shops, **Chilham**
Ye Olde England PH, **Shalmsford Street**
Compasses PH 🍺, **Sole Street**

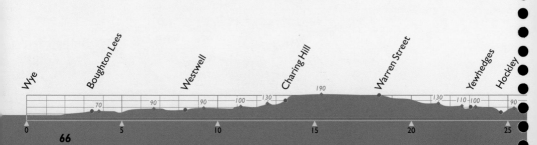

### Wye 1

There are good views across the Stour Valley from this unspoilt market town. The Church of St Gregory and St Martin houses some interesting collections. Also interesting is Wye College, founded in the 15th century by John Kempe (who later became Archbishop of Canterbury) and now an agricultural college.

### Agricultural Museum, Brook 1

Slightly off the route, a wide collection of farm implements is displayed in a 14th-century tithe barn and a 19th-century oast house.

▲ Chilham Castle

### Doddington Place Gardens 4

Beautiful rhododendrons and azaleas, a sunken garden, a rock garden and expansive lawns can be found within these 10 acres of landscaped garden.

### Chilham 20-21

The village grew up around the gates of the medieval castle. The central square is dominated by St Mary's Church and narrow streets full of pretty cottages lead off from this.

### Chilham Castle 20

Only the octagonal keep remains of the original Norman castle; the present castle was completed in 1616 and stands between the medieval ruins and the village and is not open to the public. The large gardens contain a lake, a rose garden, a deer park and a 'petland' for children.

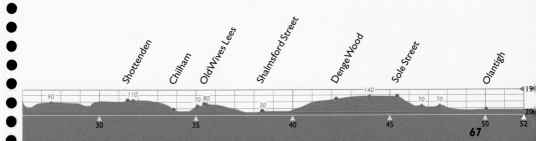

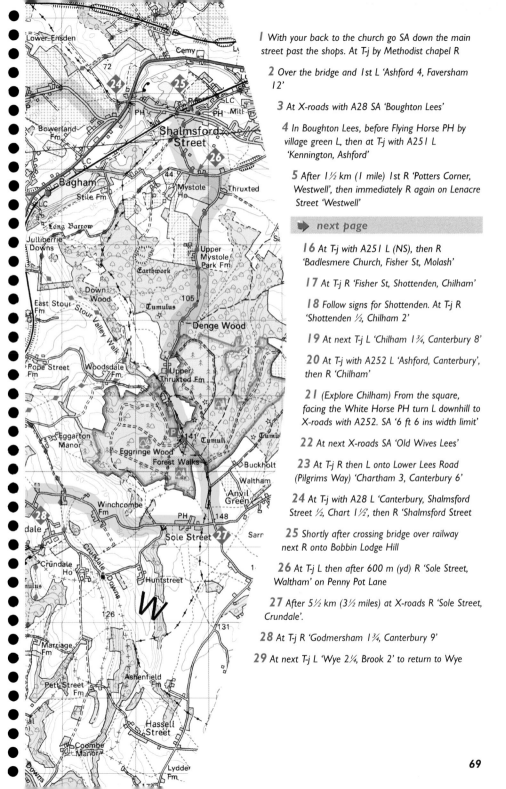

*1* With your back to the church go SA down the main street past the shops. At T-j by Methodist chapel R

*2* Over the bridge and 1st L 'Ashford 4, Faversham 12'

*3* At X-roads with A28 SA 'Boughton Lees'

*4* In Boughton Lees, before Flying Horse PH by village green L, then at T-j with A251 L 'Kennington, Ashford'

*5* After 1½ km (1 mile) 1st R 'Potters Corner, Westwell', then immediately R again on Lenacre Street 'Westwell'

➡ *next page*

*16* At T-j with A251 L (NS), then R 'Badlesmere Church, Fisher St, Molash'

*17* At T-j R 'Fisher St, Shottenden, Chilham'

*18* Follow signs for Shottenden. At T-j R 'Shottenden ½, Chilham 2'

*19* At next T-j L 'Chilham 1¾, Canterbury 8'

*20* At T-j with A252 L 'Ashford, Canterbury', then R 'Chilham'

*21* (Explore Chilham) From the square, facing the White Horse PH turn L downhill to X-roads with A252. SA '6 ft 6 ins width limit'

*22* At next X-roads SA 'Old Wives Lees'

*23* At T-j R then L onto Lower Lees Road (Pilgrims Way) 'Chartham 3, Canterbury 6'

*24* At T-j with A28 L 'Canterbury, Shalmsford Street ½, Chart 1½', then R 'Shalmsford Street

*25* Shortly after crossing bridge over railway next R onto Bobbin Lodge Hill

*26* At T-j L then after 600 m (yd) R 'Sole Street, Waltham' on Penny Pot Lane

*27* After 5½ km (3½ miles) at X-roads R 'Sole Street, Crundale'.

*28* At T-j R 'Godmersham 1¾, Canterbury 9'

*29* At next T-j L 'Wye 2¼, Brook 2' to return to Wye

**4** In Boughton Lees, before Flying Horse PH by village green L, then at T-j with A251 L 'Kennington, Ashford'

**5** After 1½ km (1 mile) 1st R 'Potters Corner, Westwell', then immediately R again on Lenacre Street 'Westwell'

**6** In Westwell at offset X-roads SA 'Charing 3¾, Maidstone 16¼'

**7** After 1½ km (1 mile) 2nd R on LH bend just after large red-brick house 'Charing'

**8** At T-j after 2½ km (1½ miles) R (NS)

**9** At T-j with A252 at the end of Pett Lane R, then 1st L on The Wynd (very steep), then at T-j L

**10** At X-roads near Bowl Inn PH SA 'Warren Street 2, Lenham 4'

**11** At T-j at end of Wareditch Road R 'Stalisfield 2¾'

**12** After 5 km (3 miles), shortly after passing, on your left, a turning to Newnham and Doddington by a large oak tree and then Wingfield Farm take next R (NS)

**13** At T-j R 'Throwley, Sheldwich'

**14** At T-j L 'Throwley 1¼, Sheldwich 3, Faversham 5', then 1st R 'Belmont ¾, Throwley 1, Sheldwich 2'

**15** After 1 km (¾ mile), on sharp RH bend L 'Badlesmere, Sheldwich'

**16** At T-j with A251 L (NS), then R 'Badlesmere Church, Fisher St, Molash'

**17** At T-j R 'Fisher St, Shottenden, Chilham'

◀ previous page

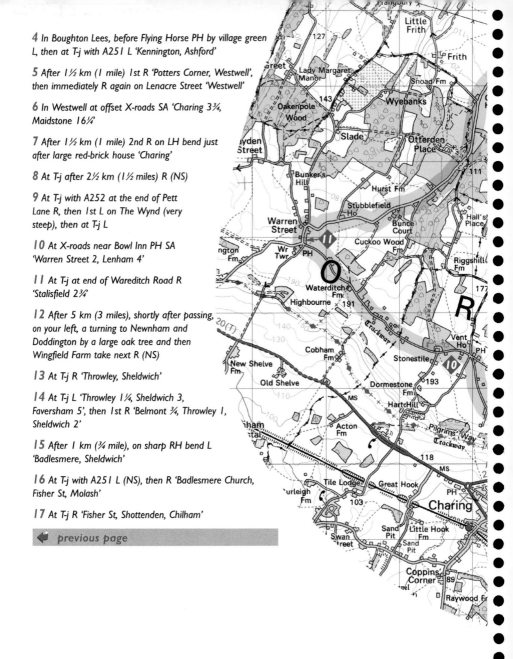

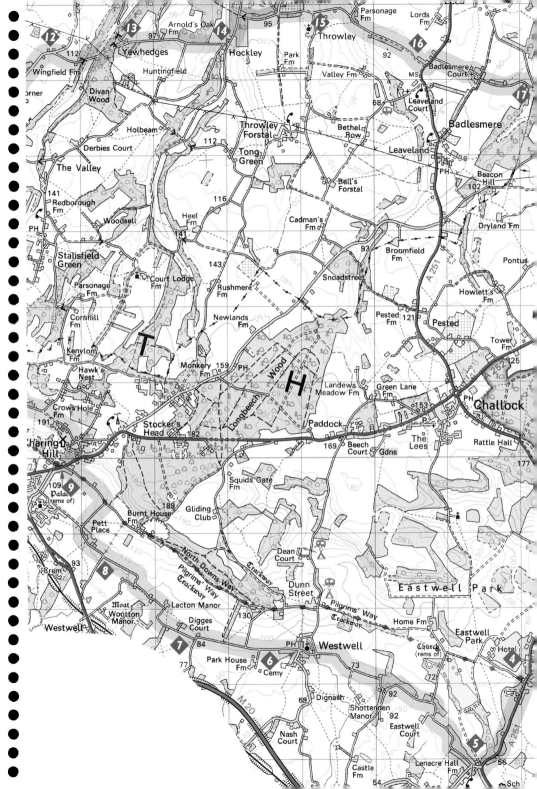

# South from Balcombe to the South Downs below Ditchling Beacon

**B**alcombe is a small village north of Haywards Heath situated on the mainline railway from London and so a far easier starting point than Haywards Heath. Immediately into the heart of attractive Sussex countryside, the ride starts with fast descents and steep climbs either side of Ardingly Reservoir. Haywards Heath is skirted around and soon after crossing the A272, the South Downs appear on the horizon. The ride heads almost due south on quiet lanes, with views towards the steep chalk escarpment of the South Downs, rising to over 213 m (700 ft) at Ditchling Beacon. You are not asked to emulate the London to Brighton charity riders who climb up over Ditchling Beacon: content yourself with the views as you turn west along the foot of the hills to Clayton. After a crossing of the busy A273, more quiet lanes take you north past Hurstpierpoint College down into the Adur Valley before climbing back up to Balcombe.

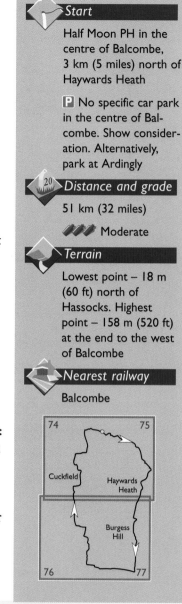

### Start

Half Moon PH in the centre of Balcombe, 3 km (5 miles) north of Haywards Heath

**P** No specific car park in the centre of Balcombe. Show consideration. Alternatively, park at Ardingly

### Distance and grade

51 km (32 miles)

Moderate

### Terrain

Lowest point – 18 m (60 ft) north of Hassocks. Highest point – 158 m (520 ft) at the end to the west of Balcombe

### Nearest railway

Balcombe

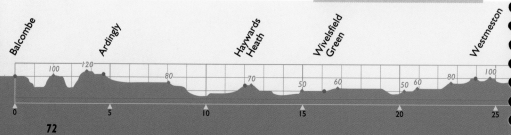

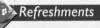
**Wakehurst Place** 4
Garden for all seasons with rare and exotic trees and shrubs. There are walks through a wooded valley, and around lakes and a bog garden

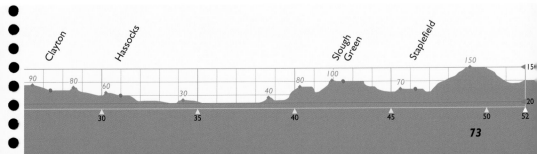

▲▼ *Wakehurst Place*

### Refreshments

*Half Moon PH,* **Balcombe**
*Gardeners Arms PH ☕, Oak at Ardingly PH ☕, Ardingly Inn PH,* **Ardingly**
*Cock PH ☕,* **Wivelsfield Green**
*Victory Inn PH ☕, Jolly Tanner PH ☕,* **Staplefield**

**Bluebell Railway** 4/5 *(off the route)*
Steam engines run on the 8 km (5 mile) line between Horsted Keynes, an old village with a spacious green that was once the centre of the medieval iron industry, and Sheffield Park with its period railway station. There is a collection of locomotives and rolling stock dating between 1865 and 1958

**1** With back to the Half Moon PH bear L 'Ardingly, Haywards Heath, Lindfield'

**2** 1st L after Police Station onto Mill Lane 'Ardingly 2¾'

**3** At T-j by letter box and triangle of grass R 'Ardingly'. Two steep climbs either side of reservoir

**4** At T-j in Ardingly L then immediately R onto B2028 'Lindfield, Haywards Heath'

**5** Busy section. Ignore 1st left to West Hoathly and the Bluebell Line. Take the next L onto Stone Cross Lane 'Horsted Keynes 2, Danehill 3½'

**6** At T-j by triangle of grass at the end of Stone Cross Lane R 'Lindfield 1¾, Haywards Heath 3 ¾' then shortly 1st L onto Plummerden Lane 'Freshfield 1¾, Sheffield Park 4, North Common 5'

**7** At T-j by triangle of grass R 'Walstead, Linfield, Haywards Heath'

**8** After 2½ km (1½ miles) at the end of the cemetery to the right bear L (NS)

**9** At T-j with B2111 L 'Scaynes Hill 1, Uckfield 11¼, Lewes 10¾'

**10** Shortly, at T-j with A272 R 'Haywards Heath' then 1st L onto Slugwash Lane '7.5 ton weight limit'

➡ **two pages**

**24** At X-roads with A272 at the end of Stairbridge Lane SA onto Buncton Lane

**25** At T-j at the top of steady climb by triangle of grass R 'Cuckfield, Ansty'

**26** At T-j with the B2115 at the end of Broxmead Lane L 'Warninglid 2' then after 800 m (½ mile) 1st R '6 ft 6 in width limit'

**27** At X-roads at the end of Staplefield Lane R (NS)

**28** At X-roads just past Victory Inn SA 'Brantridge Lane'

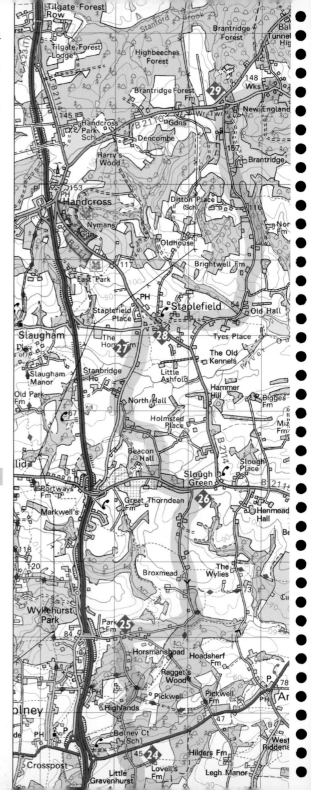

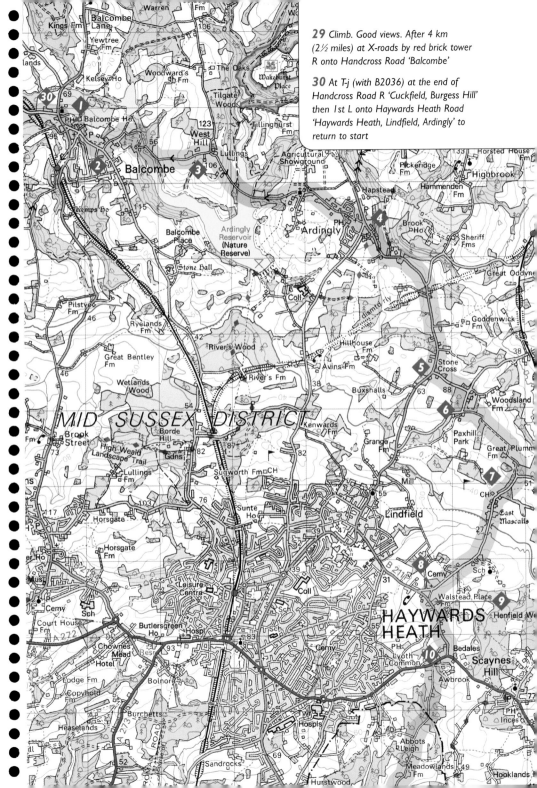

**29** Climb. Good views. After 4 km (2½ miles) at X-roads by red brick tower R onto Handcross Road 'Balcombe'

**30** At T-j (with B2036) at the end of Handcross Road R 'Cuckfield, Burgess Hill' then 1st L onto Haywards Heath Road 'Haywards Heath, Lindfield, Ardingly' to return to start

**11** After 4 km (2½ miles) at T-j at the end of Slugwash Lane L then 1st R (NS). Shortly 1st R onto Hundred Acre Lane 'Streat 3, Westmeston 5'

**12** At T-j L 'Streat 1½, Westmeston 3½' then R (same sign)

**13** At T-j with B2116 at the end of Streat Lane R 'Westmeston ¾, Ditchling 2¼, Hassocks 4'

**14** On sharp RH bend by church in Westmeston bear L (in effect SA) 'Underhill Lane, Narrow Road'

**15** At X-roads SA (same sign)

**16** At T-j with A273 at the end of Underhill Lane R then 1st L onto New Way Lane

**17** At T-j with Randiddles Close L. At end of New Way Lane R onto Hassocks Road then 1st L onto College Lane 'Hurstpierpoint College'

**18** Immediately after school L onto Chalkers Lane 'Hurstpierpoint'

**19** After 800 m (½ mile) on sharp LH bend 1st R onto Danworth Lane

**20** Cross stream, climb hill. At top 1st L onto Pomper Lane

**21** At X-roads SA onto continuation of Pomper Lane

**22** At T-j at the end of Pomper Lane L then after 800 m (½ mile) 1st R

**23** At X-roads SA 'Stairbridge Lane'

**24** At X-roads with A272 at the end of Stairbridge Lane SA onto Buncton Lane

◀ **two pages**

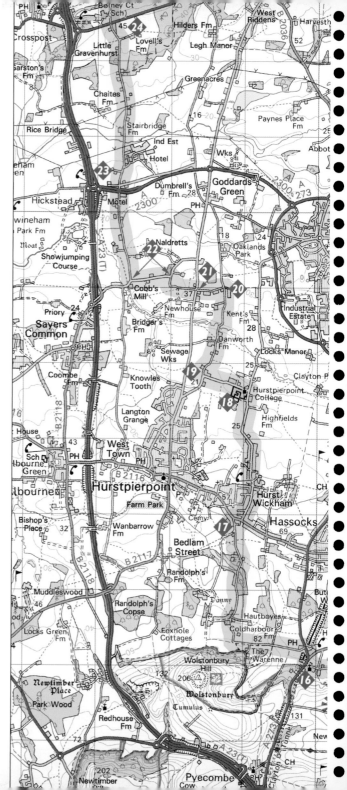

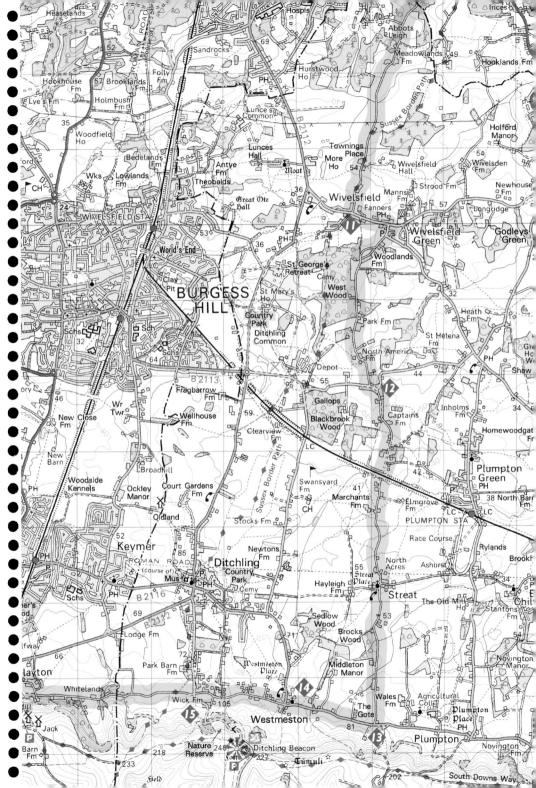

# 13 Ruined castles, Roman villas and rough riding west and north of Storrington

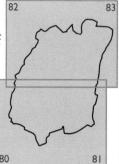

There are two points of interest in the early part of this varied ride: the ruined castle and the whole village of Amberley and the Roman villa at Bignor. Amberley, a delightful quiet backwater nestling beneath the South Downs, has many fine examples of houses built from a wide selection of materials. The ride proceeds northwards and neatly avoids spending any time on the A283 by taking a rough but rideable track east of Byworth for a short distance. Passing through various stretches of woodland, the ride describes a loop around Billingshurst before returning to Storrington on quiet lanes.

**Start**

The White Horse Hotel in the centre of Storrington

P Near the library

**Distance and grade**

53 km (33 miles)

Easy/moderate

**Terrain**

Fairly flat or undulating. One climb of 100 m (330 ft) from Shopham Bridge over the River Rother south of Byworth to Flexham Park

**Nearest railway**

Amberley

**Refreshments**

Lots of choice in **Storrington**
The Sportsman PH 🍴, The Black Horse PH 🍴, Bridge PH 🍴, tea room, **Amberley**
George and Dragon PH 🍴🍴, **Houghton**
Black Dog and Duck PH 🍴, **Bury**
White Horse PH, **Sutton**
Black Horse PH 🍴🍴 (just off the route),
Well Diggers PH, **Byworth**
Foresters PH 🍴, Half Moon PH 🍴, **Kirdford** (just off the route)
Well Diggers PH, **Byworth**
Cricketers Arms PH, **Wisborough Green**
Bat and Ball Inn, **Newpound Common**
Queens Head PH, **West Chiltington**

### Parham House, Pulborough 3-4

Built in the late 16th century but with 18th-century additions, this grey stone, gabled house lies in an ancient deer park. The gardens were designed more recently and include walled gardens, a fountain and red water-lily pond and a temple garden. Inside the house are original carved panellings and Tudor and Jacobean furniture.

### Amberley 6

An attractive village with twisting streets full of a variety of cottages, thatched, timbered, brick, stone and flint. The ruins of Amberley Castle, a former retreat of the Bishop of Chichester, and a Norman church stand on the edge of the village. The old Black Horse Inn is practically a museum with its collections of sheep bells and shepherds' crooks.

▼ Mosaic floor at Bignor

### Amberley Chalk Pits Museum 6-7

This huge industrial museum is set in a 36-acre former chalk quarry with much of the original machinery on display. Other crafts and industries are demonstrated in workshops and visitors can travel around the area on the narrow gauge railway or the workmen's train.

### Bignor 11

Some of the finest mosaic floors discovered outside Italy can be seen in the remains of this large Roman villa. The museum is also interesting and the surrounding countryside is beautiful.

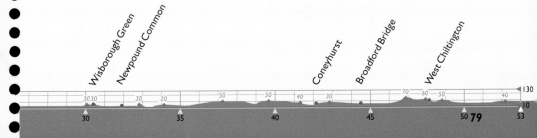

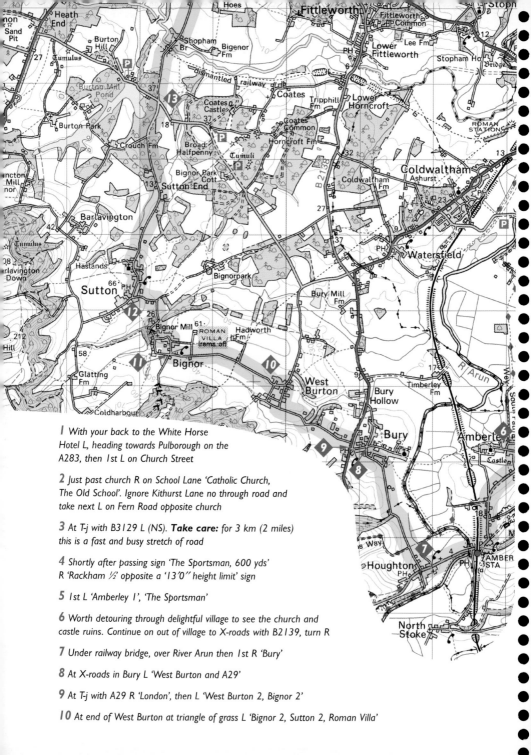

**1** With your back to the White Horse Hotel L, heading towards Pulborough on the A283, then 1st L on Church Street

**2** Just past church R on School Lane 'Catholic Church, The Old School'. Ignore Kithurst Lane no through road and take next L on Fern Road opposite church

**3** At T-j with B3129 L (NS). **Take care:** for 3 km (2 miles) this is a fast and busy stretch of road

**4** Shortly after passing sign 'The Sportsman, 600 yds' R 'Rackham ½' opposite a '13′0″' height limit' sign

**5** 1st L 'Amberley 1', 'The Sportsman'

**6** Worth detouring through delightful village to see the church and castle ruins. Continue on out of village to X-roads with B2139, turn R

**7** Under railway bridge, over River Arun then 1st R 'Bury'

**8** At X-roads in Bury L 'West Burton and A29'

**9** At T-j with A29 R 'London', then L 'West Burton 2, Bignor 2'

**10** At end of West Burton at triangle of grass L 'Bignor 2, Sutton 2, Roman Villa'

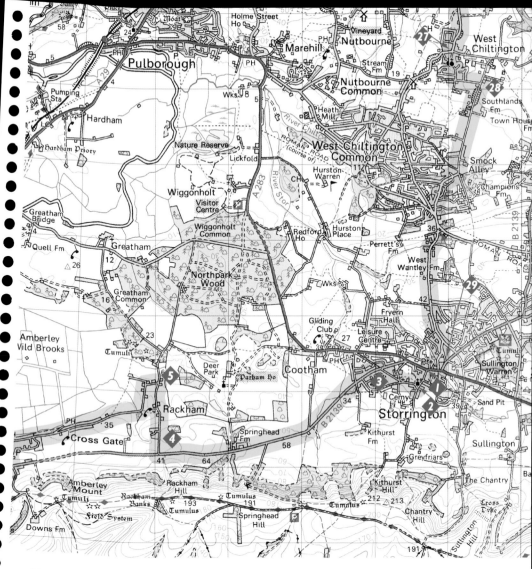

11  In Bignor follow signs for 'Sutton, Duncton'

12  At the White Horse PH in Sutton follow road uphill 'Byworth, Petworth'

13  At X-roads SA 'Petworth 3'

➡ next page

27  At X-roads in West Chiltington by Queens Head PH SA onto Church Street

28  At T-j R on Southlands Lane

29  This road becomes Smock Alley then Roundabout Lane and passes Five Bells PH. At T-j L (sign vandalized), then at T-j with B2139 R to return to Storrington

**14** At offset X-roads SA 'Byworth'

**15** **Easy to miss**. Just past brow of hill in Byworth, opposite stone and red-brick barn with large grey wooden doors R onto **track** through farm. The track is rideable

**16** Emerge at X-roads on A283 by Well Diggers PH. SA (NS)

**17** Follow signs for 'Kirdford, Plaistow'. At X-roads with A272 SA 'Plaistow 6'

**18** In Kirdford, just past Half Moon PH follow road round 'Wisborough Green 2'

**19** At X-roads in Wisborough Green SA 'Newpound'

**20** At T-j with B2133 R (NS)

**21** At T-j with A272 L 'Billingshurst', then 1st L after bridge 'Gallery 2'

**22** Ignore 1st right to Tedfold Stud Farm. Go under power lines and into wood. 800 m (½ mile) after start of wood 1st R 'Gallery ½'

**23** At T-j with A29 R 'Billingshurst 1, (use pavement/cyclepath), then 2nd L 'Barns Green 3'

**24** At T-j R 'Coneyhurst 2'

**25** At T-j with A272 L 'Cowfold', then 1st R by telephone box onto West Chiltington Lane

**26** At T-j with B2133 L 'Thakeham, Ashington', then 1st R on Broadford Bridge Road 'West Chiltington'

◀ previous page

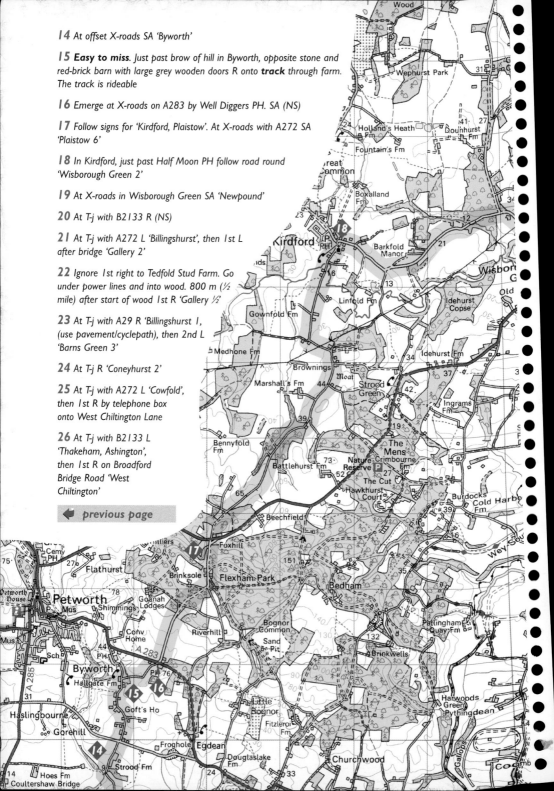

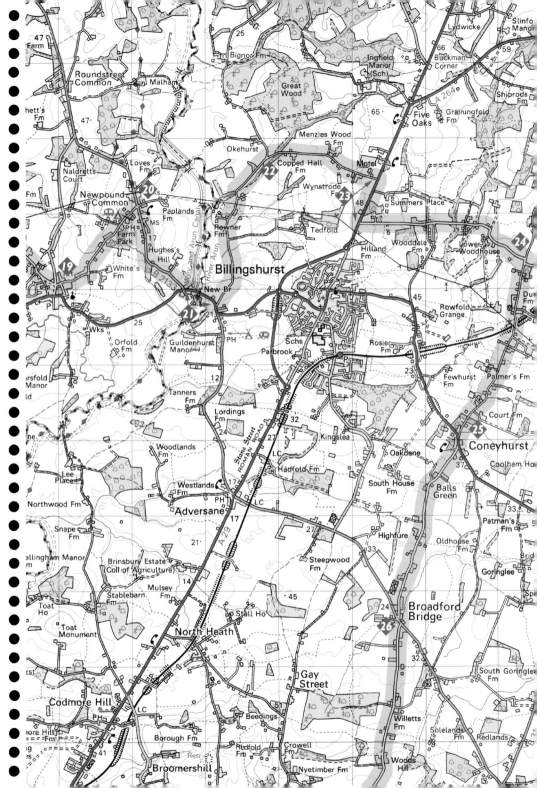

# 14 Rolling woodland northeast of Midhurst

There is easy cycling on quiet lanes north of the South Downs. This ride links the historic towns of Midhurst and Petworth via a loop through wooded lanes and small villages such as Lodsworth and Plaistow. There are many good pubs along the way and the chance of a tea stop in Petworth or back at Midhurst.

## Refreshments

Plenty of choice in **Midhurst** and **Petworth**
Three Moles PH, **Selham**
Stag Inn, **Balls Cross** Sun Inn, **Plaistow**
Lickfold Inn ●●, **Lickfold**

## Start

Knockhundred Road, by the building society in the centre of Midhurst

P Free long-term parking on the A286 Haslemere Road, going north out of Midhurst

## Distance and grade

54 km (34 miles)
Easy/moderate

## Terrain

In general, flat or undulating, but with two hills of 76 m (250 ft) in the first half of the ride, one from South Ambersham to the top of Leggatt Hill and one from Lickfold onto Shopp Hill

## Nearest railway

Haslemere, 5 km (3 miles) from the route at Gospel Green, or Billingshurst, 10 km (6 miles) from the route at Kirdford

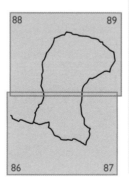

| 88 | 89 |
|---|---|
| 86 | 87 |

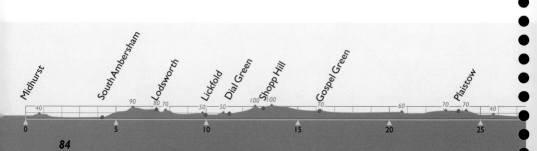

### Cowdray House 2-3

Originally known as La Coudraye, this house was the residence of
the de Bohun family when they left the castle at Midhurst.
Construction began in 1530 and, despite a fire in 1793 that left the
house a standing ruin, it is an impressive example of Tudor archi-
tecture.

### Lodsworth 6 and Lickfold 7-8

These villages are typical of the area and are surrounded and
bounded by streams and woods. Lodsworth has a charming
collection of characterful houses and cottages.

### Kirdford 13

A peaceful village with a 12th-century church and tiled cottages. In
the 16th century, it was industrially important with forges and
foundries, but this is now hard to believe.

### Petworth House and Park 15-17

This magnificent house was built by Charles Seymour, 6th Duke of
Somerset, in the late 17th century. Inside the house are some
fascinating exhibitions and the North Gallery contains a very
important collection of paintings, which includes works by Turner
(who was a visitor here), Gainsborough and Van Dyke. The 700
acres of deer park were beautifully landscaped by 'Capability'
Brown.

Balls Cross · Gunter's Bridge · Petworth · Haslingbourne · Heath End · Selham · South Ambersham

30 · 50 · 60 · 30 · 20 · 30 · 40 · 30 · 40 · 30 · 40 · 100 · 10

30 · 35 · 40 · 45 · 50 · 55

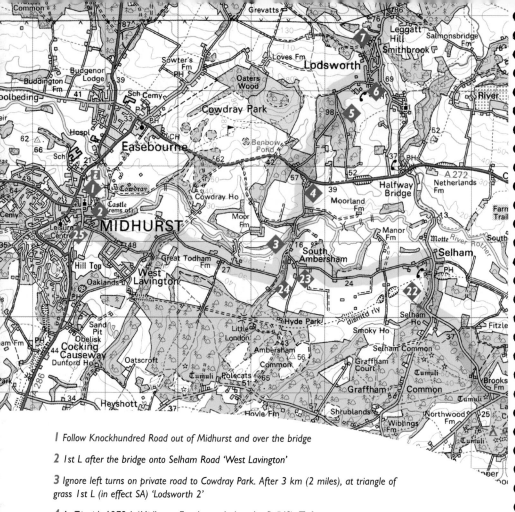

*1* Follow Knockhundred Road out of Midhurst and over the bridge

*2* 1st L after the bridge onto Selham Road 'West Lavington'

*3* Ignore left turns on private road to Cowdray Park. After 3 km (2 miles), at triangle of grass 1st L (in effect SA) 'Lodsworth 2'

*4* At T-j with A272 L 'Midhurst, Easebourne', then 1st R (NS). **Take care**

*5* At T-j at top of hill bear L (NS)

*6* At 'Lodsworth' sign 1st L on School Lane, then shortly afterwards L again, following School Lane

*7* At T-j with Myrtle Cottage ahead L (NS)

➡ **two pages**

*15* At T-j with A283 L (NS)

*16* In Petworth, follow signs for Pulborough A283 until reaching X-roads

*17* At X-roads with New Street SA onto Middle Street then at T-j after 100 m (yd) L onto High Street

*18* At T-j at end of Grove Lane after almost 1½ km (1 mile) L 'Fittleworth'

*19* 1st R at X-roads, 'Sutton'

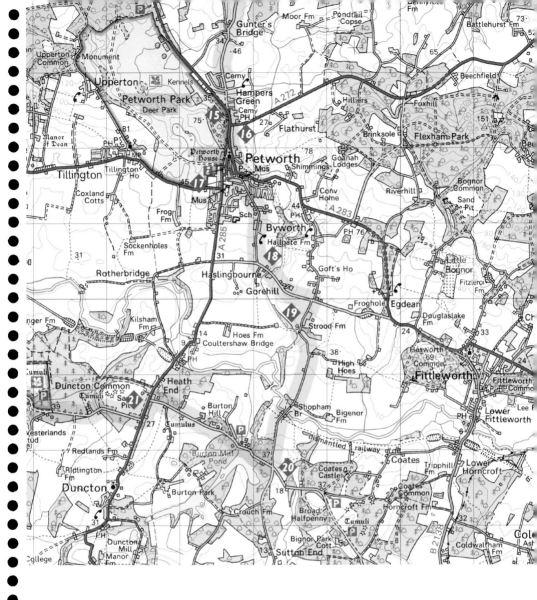

**20** At X-roads R 'Duncton'

**21** At T-j with A285 L 'Chichester 12, Duncton', then 1st R 'Selham 3 Graffham 3'

**22** At T-j R 'Mihurst 5'. Just after Three Moles PH in Selham L 'South Ambersham, Midhurst'

**23** At T-j R 'Midhurst 3, Lodsworth 3'

**24** At triangle of grass L 'West Lavington 1, Midhurst 3'

**25** Follow outward route back to start, turning R at T-j to cross bridge back into the centre of Midhurst

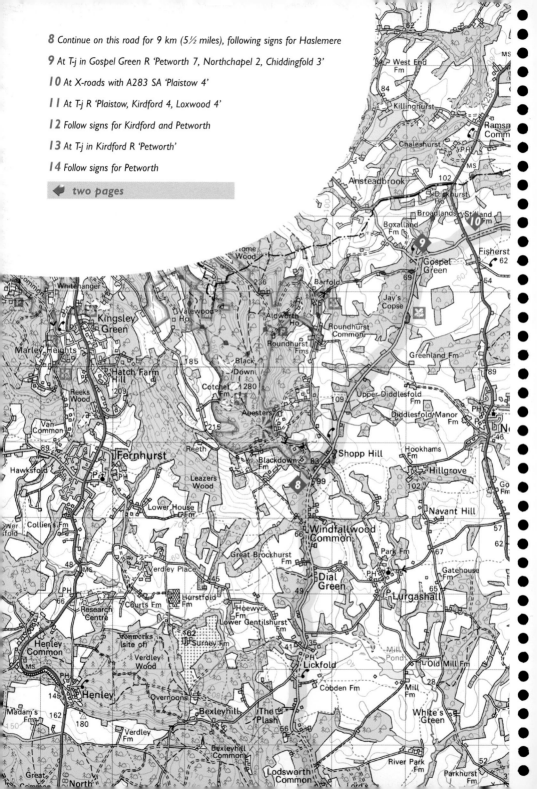

**8** *Continue on this road for 9 km (5½ miles), following signs for Haslemere*

**9** *At T-j in Gospel Green R 'Petworth 7, Northchapel 2, Chiddingfold 3'*

**10** *At X-roads with A283 SA 'Plaistow 4'*

**11** *At T-j R 'Plaistow, Kirdford 4, Loxwood 4'*

**12** *Follow signs for Kirdford and Petworth*

**13** *At T-j in Kirdford R 'Petworth'*

**14** *Follow signs for Petworth*

◀ **two pages**

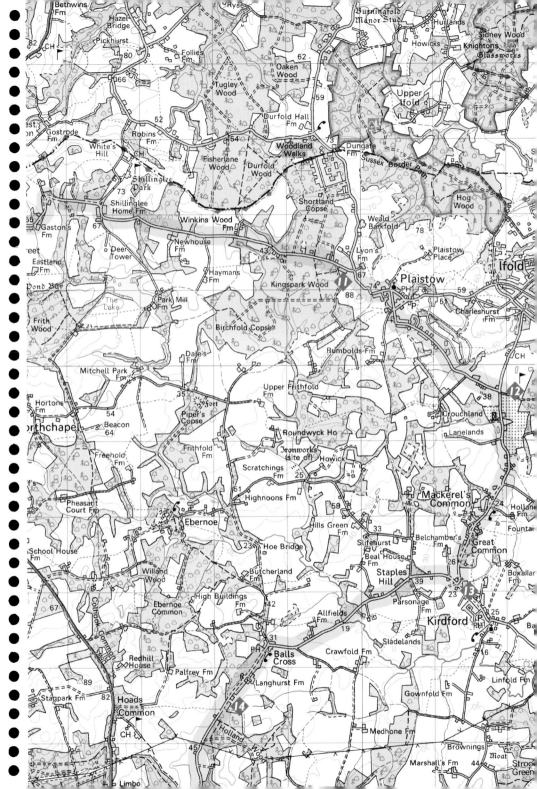

# 15 Midhurst to Petersfield and back along the foot of the South Downs

The route leaves the valley of the River Rother, taking some impressive sunken lanes through woods north to Milland. It is worth stopping there to look at the beautiful work produced by The Living Tree, including

94          95

92          93

wooden toys from all over the world. The ride climbs to cross the A3 at Hill Brow and sweeps down through Liss to come around the back of Petersfield. Around the large square in Petersfield, there are many watering holes and attractive Georgian houses. Having left the B2146 at Nursted, the ride is an absolute dream of quiet flat lanes beneath the folds of the South Downs back to Midhurst.

### Start

The Silver Shoe PH, High St, Midhurst

P Heading north out of town on the A286

### Distance and grade

45 km (28 miles)

Moderate

### Terrain

Three climbs: 91 m (300 ft )between Midhurst and Milland, 91 m (300 ft) from Milland to Hill Brow on the A3, 79 m (260 ft) from Liss to Bushy Hill. Flat from Petersfield back to Midhurst

### Nearest railway

Petersfield

### Refreshments

Spread Eagle PH 🍺🍺, lots of choice, **Midhurst**
Rising Sun PH, **Milland**
Crossing Gate PH, **Liss**
Drovers PH, **Hill Brow**
Cricketers PH 🍺, Harrow PH 🍺🍺, **Steep**
Lots of choice in **Petersfield**
White Hart PH 🍺, The Ship PH, Coach and Horses PH 🍺, **South Harting**
Three Horseshoes PH 🍺🍺, **Elsted**

Midhurst · Woolbeding · Robins · Milland · Hill Brow · Liss · Bushy Hill · Steep

50   60   50   110   70   70   100   140   80   130   100

0        5        10        15        20

 **Places of interest**

### Midhurst 1
The origins of this town lie in the early Middle Ages when the Norman Lord, Savaric Fitzcane, built a castle on St Anne's Hill. This castle is now completely ruined but there are many other buildings that display Midhurst's history.

### Midhurst Parish Church
This church and its beautiful churchyard overlook the Market Square

### Market Hall, Town Hall and The Spread Eagle
The timber building in front of the Spread Eagle is the 16th-century Market Hall where the Grammar School was founded in 1672. The Town Hall dates from the early 19th century and still has the stocks and lock up. The Spread Eagle is one of the most impressive buildings in the town.

### Petersfield 16
Once an important town for the wool trade, Petersfield is now a busy market town. A statue of William III guards the central square and there is a large lake southeast of the town.

Petersfield    Nursted    Quebec    Elsted    Treyford    Bepton

80    80    90    90    80    80    90    80    60    140    30

25    30    35    40    45

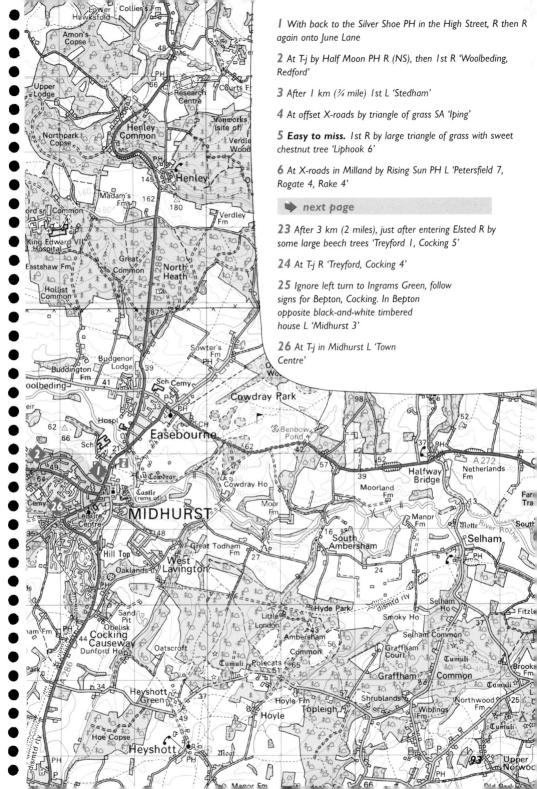

**1** With back to the Silver Shoe PH in the High Street, R then R again onto June Lane

**2** At T-j by Half Moon PH R (NS), then 1st R 'Woolbeding, Redford'

**3** After 1 km (¾ mile) 1st L 'Stedham'

**4** At offset X-roads by triangle of grass SA 'Iping'

**5** **Easy to miss.** 1st R by large triangle of grass with sweet chestnut tree 'Liphook 6'

**6** At X-roads in Milland by Rising Sun PH L 'Petersfield 7, Rogate 4, Rake 4'

➡ *next page*

**23** After 3 km (2 miles), just after entering Elsted R by some large beech trees 'Treyford 1, Cocking 5'

**24** At T-j R 'Treyford, Cocking 4'

**25** Ignore left turn to Ingrams Green, follow signs for Bepton, Cocking. In Bepton opposite black-and-white timbered house L 'Midhurst 3'

**26** At T-j in Midhurst L 'Town Centre'

**7** *Continue on this road for 5 km (3 miles) following signs for Petersfield through X-roads at the top of hill*

**8** *At T-j R uphill 'Petersfield 3, Liss 1'*

**9** *At offset X-roads with the B2070 by the Drovers PH, SA onto B3006 'Liss 1'*

**10** *Through Liss, crossing railway line. At T-j with A325 R 'Farnham, Alton', then 1st L 'Hawkley 2, Priors Dean 3'*

**11** *After 1½ km (1 mile) 1st L 'Wheatham, Steep Marsh'*

**12** *Up steep hill. At T-j L 'Steep, Petersfield' and follow signs for Steep for 2½ km (1½ miles), ignoring left and right turns*

**13** *Where Mill Lane ends at T-j R (NS)*

**14** *At T-j by The Cricketeers PH L 'Petersfield'*

**15** *At roundabout L 'Town Centre, Midhurst 11'*

**16** *After crossing railway lines 2nd R onto Chapel Street*

**17** *At T-j at end of High Street by the war memorial R then after 300 m (yd) L by filling station onto Sussex Road 'South Harting B2146'*

**18** *After almost 3 km (2 miles), shortly after going under power lines, on sharp RH bend L by triangle of grass (NS)*

**19** *1st R 'West Harting'*

**20** *At T-j R 'South Harting 2', then 1st L 'West Harting'*

**21** *At T-j R 'South Harting'. At next T-j R 'South Harting'*

**22** *At T-j in South Harting L 'Midhurst, Elsted'*

**23** *After 3 km (2 miles), just after entering Elsted R by some large beech trees 'Treyford 1, Cocking 5'*

◀ **previous page**

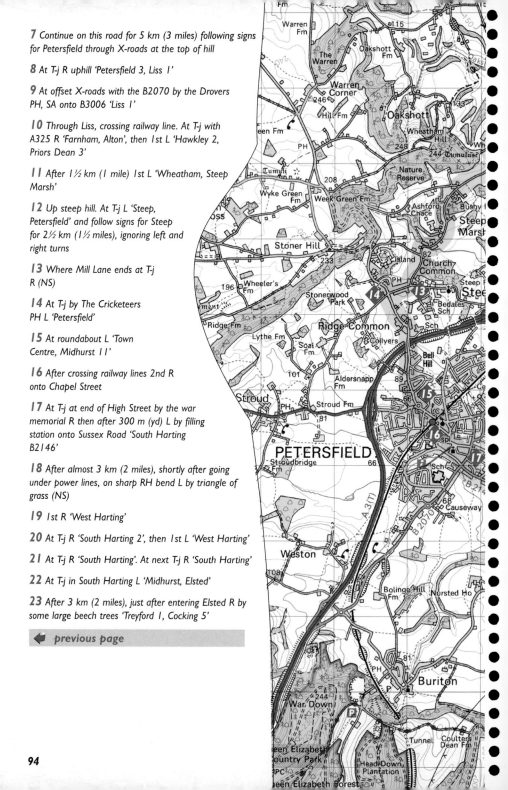

# Rolling hills and woodland north from New Alresford to Odiham

Gentle hills and woodlands are the setting for this ride in the very heart of Hampshire. New Alresford is an attractive small town with fine wide avenues and plenty in the way of refreshment. The ride passes through open countryside and woodland and few villages of any size until reaching Odiham, another town with a broad main street flanked by old brick houses. The return trip passes through similar scenery but takes in the three typical Hampshire villages of Bentworth, Medstead and Bighton.

 **Start**

Horse and Groom PH, Broad Street, New Alresford

P New Alresford station car park

**Distance and grade**

60 km (38 miles)

Moderate

 **Terrain**

Mainly undulating. Despite climbs of 85 m (280 ft) to Bugmore Hill, 76 m (250 ft) between Preston Candover and Herriard, 120 m (400 ft) south from Odiham towards Golden Pot and 70 m (230 ft) between Shalden and Medstead, all the hills are fairly gentle

**Nearest railway**

Limited service on the Midhants Watercress Line from Alton to New Alresford or Alton, 5 km (3 miles) from Golden Pot, or Hook, 5 km (3 miles) from Odiham

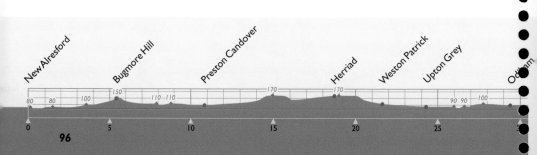

▲ New Alresford

 Refreshments

Horse and Groom PH 🍺🍺, lots of choice in **New Alresford**
Haddington Arms PH 🍺, **Upton Grey**
The George PH 🍺 (also does cream teas),
The Bell PH, **Odiham**
The Golden Pot PH, **Golden Pot**
The Sun PH 🍺🍺, **Bentworth**
Castle of Comfort PH, **Medstead**
Three Horse Shoes PH 🍺, **Bighton**

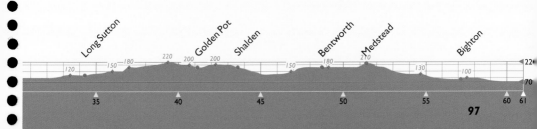

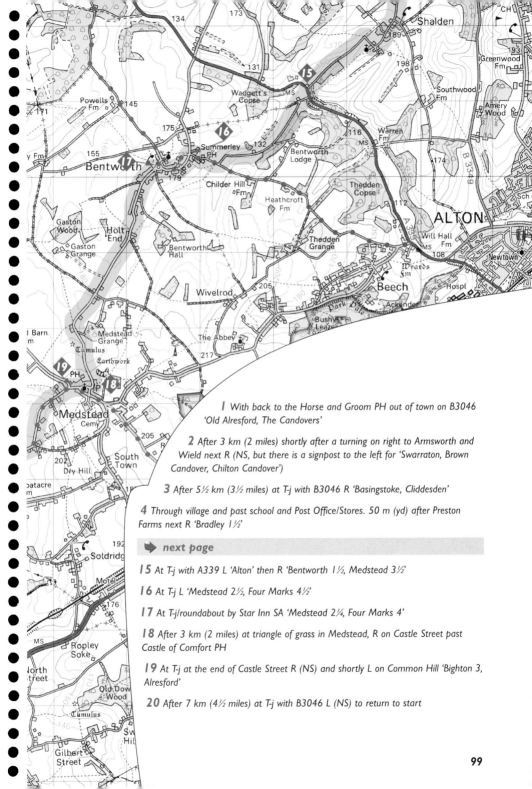

**1** With back to the Horse and Groom PH out of town on B3046 'Old Alresford, The Candovers'

**2** After 3 km (2 miles) shortly after a turning on right to Armsworth and Wield next R (NS, but there is a signpost to the left for 'Swarraton, Brown Candover, Chilton Candover')

**3** After 5½ km (3½ miles) at T-j with B3046 R 'Basingstoke, Cliddesden'

**4** Through village and past school and Post Office/Stores. 50 m (yd) after Preston Farms next R 'Bradley 1½'

➡ *next page*

**15** At T-j with A339 L 'Alton' then R 'Bentworth 1½, Medstead 3½'

**16** At T-j L 'Medstead 2½, Four Marks 4½'

**17** At T-j/roundabout by Star Inn SA 'Medstead 2¼, Four Marks 4'

**18** After 3 km (2 miles) at triangle of grass in Medstead, R on Castle Street past Castle of Comfort PH

**19** At T-j at the end of Castle Street R (NS) and shortly L on Common Hill 'Bighton 3, Alresford'

**20** After 7 km (4½ miles) at T-j with B3046 L (NS) to return to start

**5** At T-j R 'Herriard 2, Basingstoke 3'

**6** At X-roads with A339 SA 'Weston Patrick 1½, Upton Grey 3, Odiham 6'

**7** Through Upton Grey. Just before sign for North Warnborough R 'Odiham ¾, South Warnborough 2½'

**8** On sharp LH bend just past telephone box, R onto West Street (no through road). At X-roads with B3349 SA onto High Street

**9** Next to Chinese restaurant opposite the bank R 'Long Sutton 3. Hospital, Library'

**10 Easy to miss.** After almost 3 km (2 miles), just after landing lights on left and emergency gates on right, R on small lane, following perimeter fence (NS)

**11** At T-j L 'Well', then 1st R onto Copse Lane 'Froyle 2¾'

**12** At T-j R 'Golden Pot 2¾, Herriard 6¾'

**13** At X-roads with B3349 at the Golden Pot PH SA onto The Avenue 'Shalden 1½, Lasham 2½'

**14 Easy to miss.** After 1 km (¾ mile) 1st L 'Shalden 1, Bentworth 3½'

← previous page

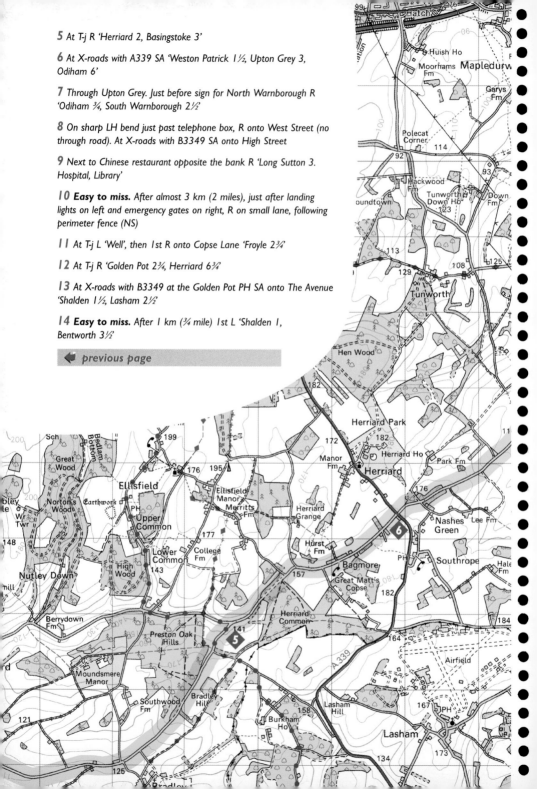

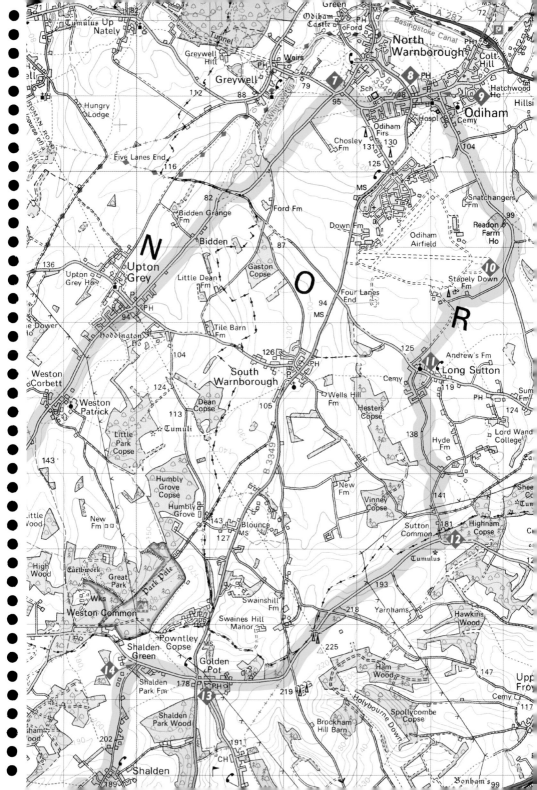

# Along the North Downs Way north of Hurst Green and Oxted

The ride starts from the railway station at Hurst Green, makes its way through Oxted and Limpsfield on quiet roads and tracks before the toughest climb of the day on a wooded track past Titsey Park to the top of Botley Hill. The descent down into Woldingham is something of a boneshaker. By contrast, what is marked as a bridleway through Marden Park is, in fact, a delightful tarmac lane along the valley bottom with no traffic. A second steep climb up onto the North Downs, beneath Gravelly Hill, is followed by a wide range of refreshment possibilities in the attractive village of Bletchingley. Beyond here, the route is a little confusing for the first kilometre (¾ mile) or so, but the general direction is eastwards on bridleways cutting across a series of roads through woodland and farmland to return to Hurst Green.

○Hurst Green

104      103

## Start

Hurst Green railway station, south of the A25 between Redhill and Westerham. (M25 junction 6)

**P** As above

## Distance and grade

32 km (20 miles)

Strenuous

## Terrain

Woodland, farmland. Two major climbs and several shorter ones – 155 m (510 ft) from the bridge beneath the M25 to the masts on Botley Hill, 122 m (400 ft) from Woldingham Garden Village to Gravelly Hill to the west of the A22. Lowest point – 79 m (260 ft) at the start. Highest point – 265 m (870 ft) at the masts on Botley Hill, southeast of Woldingham

## Nearest railway

Hurst Green

Hurst Green    M25    Botley Hill   260    Woldingham   220    Woldingham Garden Village   200    Winders Hill

150

0       5       10       15

**1** Out of Hurst Green railway station car park, turn R then immediately R again onto Oast Road 'St John's Church'. Ignore 1st right turn (The Maltings) take the next R onto Icehouse Wood

**2** Climb steadily on tarmac ignoring left and right turns. At T-j with more major road at the end of Icehouse Wood SA onto narrow tarmac track 'Bridleway' (not the right hand fork, which is a private drive)

**3** Continue in the same direction on single track over Limpsfield Common following blue arrows. Where track rejoins tarmac follow the lane SA past a red tile house with tall chimneys

**4** At T-j with road by St Michael's School, at the end of the track/lane turn L. At traffic lights with the A25 SA onto the B269 'Warlingham' then 30 m (yd) after the telephone box on the right next track R uphill 'Bridleway'. Shortly after the house fork R (blue arrow)

**5** Lovely single track through woodland. At T-j with broader track by a green metal gate L downhill. At T-j with the main road (B269) SA onto track 'Bridleway'

**6** Fine, broad, stone track beneath the M25. At X-roads by the lodge for Titsey Foundation SA uphill. Long steep climb which will probably involve some pushing. The North Downs Way joins from the left

**7** At the top of the hill, at T-j with busy road (B2024) L then L again onto The Ridge

**8** After 2 km (1¼ miles) 1st R at offset X-roads onto tarmac lane 'Bridleway'. Where the road swings right towards the mast continue SA onto track. The broad track becomes single track and continues in the same direction

➡ **two pages**

**25** Follow single track and 'Bridleway' signs in the same direction to the road at Broadham Green. At T-j L then R onto Tanhouse Road 'Hurst Green, Limpsfield'

**26** At X-roads with Woodhurst Lane SA onto Church Way. At T-j with Oast Road R then at next T-j by the green, L and L again to return to the start

**8** After 2 km (1¼ miles) 1st R at offset X-roads onto tarmac lane 'Bridleway'. Where the road swings right towards the mast continue SA onto track. The broad track becomes single track and continues in the same direction

**9** Up and over the hill. Fine views down into Woldingham. Bumpy descent. At T-j with road L

**10** At the top of steep climb opposite a row of semi-detached houses turn R sharply back on yourself onto Lunghurst Road. 1st L onto Croft Road then after 300 m (yd) opposite the church and just before joining busier road turn R onto the broad track called Long Hill

**11** Easy to miss. After 800 m (½ mile) on a fast descent keep an eye out for the track which bears off to the R 'Bridleway' (blue arrow). At T-j with tarmac lane by a house called High Shaw SA onto track. This becomes tarmac and a fast descent

**12** At T-j with road by golf course turn L downhill. At junction at the end of Slines New Road bear R (not Bug Hill) towards railway viaduct. Immediately after viaduct turn sharply L back on yourself 'Private Road, Bridleway only'

**13** Lovely lane along the valley bottom. Go past school buildings. Shortly after the tennis courts to the right bear R (in effect SA) through metal gates 'Private Road'

**14** At T-j by South Lodge R 'Bridleway'. Follow this track past vineyard, houses and large warehouse. The track turns to tarmac. 600 m (yd) after the warehouse 1st R onto broad track sharply back on yourself uphill (not the North Downs Way)

**15 Easy to miss.** As the gradient eases keep an eye out for gate/stile to the left leading to a bridge over the busy A22. Cross bridge, at road turn L uphill then immediately after passing left turn to caravan site turn L onto rough track (stone 'Bridleway' marker). The track soon improves

**16** At T-j with the road L 'North Downs Way' then after 100 m (yd) 1st L onto track 'North Downs Way'. **Easy to miss.** Shortly, turn R uphill 'North Downs Way'. The track soon forks. Stay on the upper RH fork (blue arrow)

**17** At the road L then L again after 50 m (yd) onto Hextalls Lane 'Bridleway'. At major X-roads L onto Roughets Lane then shortly after Riders Cottage on the right, take the next track R 'Bridleway' (blue arrow)

**18** Under the M25. At T-j with road bear L onto lane into Bletchingley. At X-roads with the A25 SA 'Outwood'. After 800 m (½ mile) just before the start of the downhill turn L onto broad tarmac parking space then immediately L by a metal gate 'Bridleway'

**19** Follow the main tarmac track ignoring turns. At fork shortly after tarmac ends bear R by green metal post. The next section is a little hard to follow but essentially you are continuing in the same direction of travel. At T-j with more major track turn L then bear R downhill and bear L following blue arrows

**20** At T-j with tarmac bear L (in effect SA) uphill and after 50 m (yd) fork R 'Bridleway'

**21** At T-j with road by black and white house L, then shortly after a RH bend turn R onto track 'Greensand Way, Bridleway'

**22** At road R then L 'Bridleway'. Broad track becomes single track. Follow blue arrows. At road R

**23** At T-j with busier road (B2236) R then L onto Church Lane 'Godstone Church' then 1st R onto No Through Road 'Bridleway'. Under the A22 then at T-j of tracks by Hop Garden Cottage where the main track swings left bear R onto narrower track

**24** At T-j with road with red-brick barns ahead R uphill. At T-j with more major road by a 'Give Way' sign L then R 'Tandridge Court Farm. Bridleway'. As the main track swings left into the farm bear R

**25** Follow single track and 'Bridleway' signs in the same direction to the road at Broadham Green. At T-j then R onto Tanhouse Road 'Hurst Green, Limpsfield'

◀ two pages

## Refreshments

Plenty of choice in **Oxted**
Plenty of choice in **Bletchingley**
Barley Mow PH , Brickmakers Arms PH ,
**Tandridge**
Haycutter PH, **Broadham Green**

# Through the North Downs from Walton on the Hill

It may seem unlikely that an off-road route is to be found in such a built up area but, by linking together stretches of bridleway and RUPPs, most of this ride is spent on wooded tracks which give you the illusion of being far from the traffic madness of the nearby towns, trunk roads and motorways. The ride drops down from Walton on the Hill to join the course of the old Roman road of Stane Street which used to run from London to Chichester. Headley Heath offers some fine off-road cycling but there are so many tracks that it is all but impossible to describe a route across it. The ride heads east along the steep escarpment above Reigate with wonderful views from Colley Hill. Leaving the M25 behind, you cross Walton Heath and Banstead Heath alongside the inevitable golf course back to the start.

NB A short cut is decribed from Headley back to Walton, effectively making two rides of 13 and 14 km (8 and 9 miles).

**Start**

The village pond in Walton on the Hill on the B2220 towards Tadworth. Walton on the Hill is between Reigate and Leatherhead

P No specific car park

**Distance and grade**

22 km (14 miles)

Moderate

**Terrain**

Farmland, woodland and heath. Two climbs – the first a steady 91 m (300 ft) to the top of Mickleham Downs, the second 106 m (350 ft) from

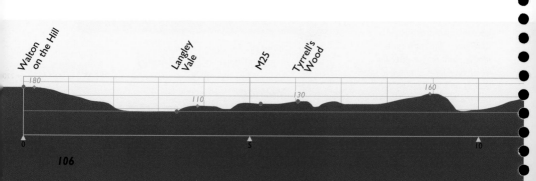

the lane in the valley between Mickleham Downs and Headley Heath up to Colley Hill. Lowest point – 79 m (260 ft) at the northern tip of the ride. Highest point – 213 m (700 ft) at Colley Hill above Reigate

### Nearest railway

Tadworth, 2 km (1¼ miles) north of the start

▼ Near Juniper Hill

### Places of interest

**Headley** 8
Yews mark the spot where Headley's 14th-century church was pulled down in the last century, and the spire of its 19th-century successor serves as a Surrey landmark. The wide expanse of wooded heath just south of Headley forms Headley Heath. There is an abundance of wildlife and a picnic area is located beside the ancient Brimmer Pond. Good family cycling here on a dense network of tracks

**Box Hill** 6 (south of the route)
Named after the box trees that grow on its flanks, Box Hill, at 171 m (563 ft) is a noted viewpoint and designated area of outstanding natural beauty, including both wood and downland scenery

**Mickleham** 3 (southwest of the route)
Playwright George Meredith was born here in 1864. Yews from a Druid's Grove Folly stand in the grounds of 18th-century Norbury Park

### Refreshments:

Chequers PH ♥, **Walton on the Hill**
Cock Horse PH ♥♥, **Headley**
Sportsmans PH, **Lower Kingswood**

Headley

Mogadon

180    190    220    200    220

90

15    20    22

**107**

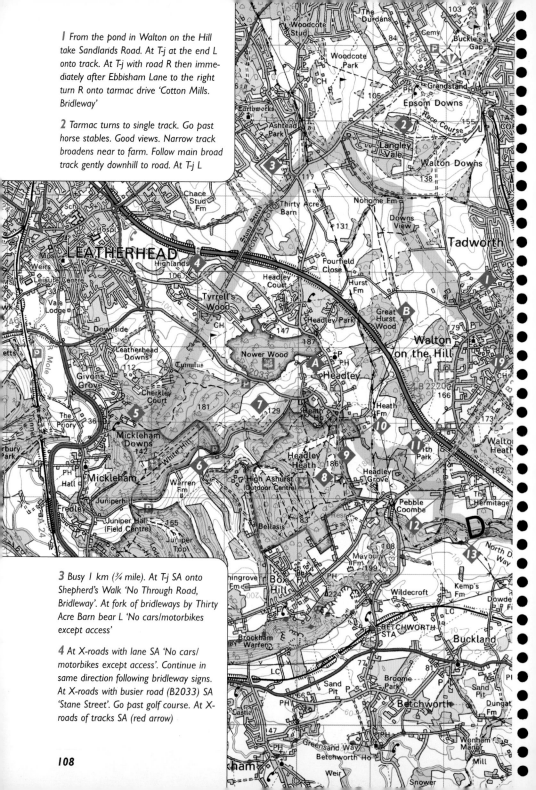

**1** *From the pond in Walton on the Hill take Sandlands Road. At T-j at the end L onto track. At T-j with road R then immediately after Ebbisham Lane to the right turn R onto tarmac drive 'Cotton Mills. Bridleway'*

**2** *Tarmac turns to single track. Go past horse stables. Good views. Narrow track broadens near to farm. Follow main broad track gently downhill to road. At T-j L*

**3** *Busy 1 km (¾ mile). At T-j SA onto Shepherd's Walk 'No Through Road, Bridleway'. At fork of bridleways by Thirty Acre Barn bear L 'No cars/motorbikes except access'*

**4** *At X-roads with lane SA 'No cars/ motorbikes except access'. Continue in same direction following bridleway signs. At X-roads with busier road (B2033) SA 'Stane Street'. Go past golf course. At X-roads of tracks SA (red arrow)*

### short cut

**Headley to Walton on the Hill**

**A** At the B2033 go SA then shortly at next X-roads SA. At T-j with road L. Shortly after Broome Close on the left take next R onto tarmac/track 'Bridleway'

**B** Go under the M25, stay in the sunken LH track. At fork L. Climb. At road R then soon after Ebbisham Lane next track L. At tarmac R onto Sandlands to return to start

**5** At fork with 'NT Mickleham Downs' sign bear L steeply uphill. **Easy to miss.** Shortly at offset X-roads of tracks turn sharp L (blue arrow) 'NT Long Walk'. This soon joins broader track along clearing with lovely views

**6** At the end of clearing, 30 m (yd) before 2 white bollards in path, turn R downhill onto narrow track 'NT Long Walk' Steep, at times technical descent. At X-roads with road by Cockshott Cottage L

**7** At T-j at the end of Lodge Bottom Road R 'Headley' then after 150 m (yd) opposite road on left turn 1st R onto Crabtree Lane 'Bridleway'. Follow track round to the R between houses (Broom House to the left)

**8** Bear L at each of three forks in the trail. Sandy track turns to gravel then tarmac. At X-roads with major road (B2033) turn R

**9** After 300 m (yd) turn L onto track opposite Headley Heath car park, to the R of National Trust overflow car park and the private drive to Wardens Cottage

**10** At X-roads with tarmac drive by White Lodge SA. At T-j by NT Headley Heath sign bear R

**11** At fork R 'Bridleway' (blue arrow). At X-roads with B2032 SA onto bridleway. At T-j by wire fence L

**12** At T-j with tarmac L then 1st R onto wide track 'Public Byway'. 100 m (yd) after track enters woodland and starts to descend 1st L (white arrow on tree)

**13** Track descends towards wood. **Easy to miss.** After following the track for 200 m (yd) alongside edge of woodland turn L uphill (white arrow on tree). Magnificent views

**14** Shortly after joining tarmac bear R just past entrance to Mount Hill 'Bridleway'

**15** At end of fenced in section with Mole Place to the right turn L onto tarmac track then after 30 m (yd) R 'North Downs Way'

**16** Shortly after views open up on a broad expanse of open downland, and 200 m (yd) before a round stone pavilion with columns, turn L sharply back on yourself by metal gate

**17** At junction by Margery Wood car park turn L. At road R then at T-j L. Where road forks right (towards Sportsmans PH) keep eye out for bridleway between wooden posts. Shortly bear R 'Bridleway, Chequers Lane' then after 200 m (yd) at X-roads of tracks R 'Bridleway, Walton on the Hill 1¼'

**18** Short rough section soon improves alongside golf course. At fork with 'Permissive Horse Ride' to the right bear L and shortly fork L again

**19** At road R then shortly L onto bridleway. Follow in the same direction eventually bearing L to join road near the Blue Ball PH in Walton on the Hill

#  Onto Leith Hill southeast from Gomshall

Leith Hill is one of the most popular areas for mountain-biking in southeast England and is probably best appreciated mid-week or out of season when there are less people about. This ride starts from Gomshall, running through the sandy soil that characterise the area to the south of the North Downs escarpment. The sand can at times be hard going, particularly after a long, dry spell, when you may find yourself pushing the bike, even on fairly flat sections. One of the few places in the country where the ride is better after rain! The farmland between Abinger Hammer and Westcott is left behind as you climb 213 m (700 ft) through mixed woodland over almost 8 km (5 miles) to the top of Leith Hill where the views are just reward for such a sustained effort. A sharp descent drops you down to the beds of clay near to the B2126. These are soon left behind as you climb once again, to the neighbouring high point of Holmbury Hill. With one short exception it is downhill all the way to Gomshall including a long, tunnel-like descent near the end.

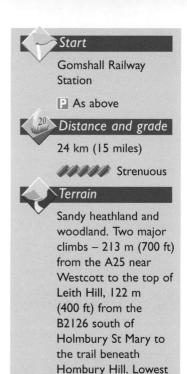

**Start**

Gomshall Railway Station

P As above

**Distance and grade**

24 km (15 miles)

Strenuous

**Terrain**

Sandy heathland and woodland. Two major climbs – 213 m (700 ft) from the A25 near Westcott to the top of Leith Hill, 122 m (400 ft) from the B2126 south of Holmbury St Mary to the trail beneath Hombury Hill. Lowest point – 76 m (250 ft) in Gomshall. Highest point – 294 m (965 ft) at the top of Leith Hill

**Nearest railway**

Gomshall

**Friday Street** 8/9 *(just off the route)*
Tiny hamlet with pine-clad hills and tranquil lake. Water once powered the bellows of the 17th-century ironworks in the surrounding forests. The Stephen Langton Inn is named after King John's Archbishop of Canterbury, born here in 1150

**Abinger Common** 9 *(just off the route)*
There are stocks on the village green, overlooked by a church dating from the 12th century. A path leads past the grounds of Abinger Manor where a small shelter covers the remains of a pit dwelling occupied about 4000 BC; perhaps the oldest man-made dwelling in Britain

**Leith Hill** 11
At 294 m (965 ft) the highest point in southeast England. The tower was built in 1766 by Richard Hull, who is buried upside down beneath the tower

**Holmbury Hill** 16
Site of an ancient fortified camp dating from 150 BC. The double banks and ditches can still be seen in places. In 1930, excavations yielded many flint tools, pottery shards and other items

▲ Leith Tower

 **Refreshments:**

Kings Head PH 🍴, **Holmbury St Mary** *(off the route at 13)*
Hurtwood PH, **Peaslake** *(1 km (¾ mile) off the route)*
Stephen Langton Inn 🍴, **Friday Street**
The Plough PH 🍴🍴, **Coldharbour**
Plenty of choice in **Gomshall**

*1* From Gomshall BR Station, cross the A25, turn L through pedestrian tunnel, then 1st R onto Wonham Way (no through road). Follow the track round to the L by Twiga Lodge

*2* On next RH bend by signpost for Southbrook Farmhouse turn L. Follow enclosed track to R of white gate for Brook Cottage. At T-j with concrete track bear R. At T-j with A25 R then 1st L after Abinger Arms PH 'No vehicles except access'

*3* At brow of hill, opposite lane on the left, turn R onto gravel track (blue arrow)

*4* At X-roads of tracks at the exit of field SA uphill (blue arrow). In large grassy clearing ignore right fork then ignore left turn. At bottom of steep hill bear L on sandy track along LH edge of woodland

*5* At T-j with road L then R 'Bridleway'. Sandy track

*6* At offset X-roads of tracks shortly after farm buildings go SA onto tarmac track

*7* At T-j with road by houses R. At T-j with A25 at the end of Balchins Lane L then R onto Rookery Drive. Follow the drive past lovely thatched house, bearing L onto track just before The Rookery

*8* Climb steeply on narrow, sunken, sandy track through woodland. At T-j at top L onto middle of three tracks. Ignore turns to left and right

*9* Long steady climb. At fork of tracks near pine plantation bear L. At T-j with road by the Plough PH in Coldharbour turn R steeply uphill on track by letterbox

*10* At fork of tracks before the cricket pavilion bear R then fork L (do not follow track around pitch to the pavilion itself). At a series of junctions continue in the same direction, maintaining or gaining height

*11* Continue past Leith Hill tower in same direction, descending and taking LH fork. At T-j with road diagonally R past Starveall Corner noticeboard and car parking area

*12* Steep descent. At X-roads of tracks (with large house to the left) go SA

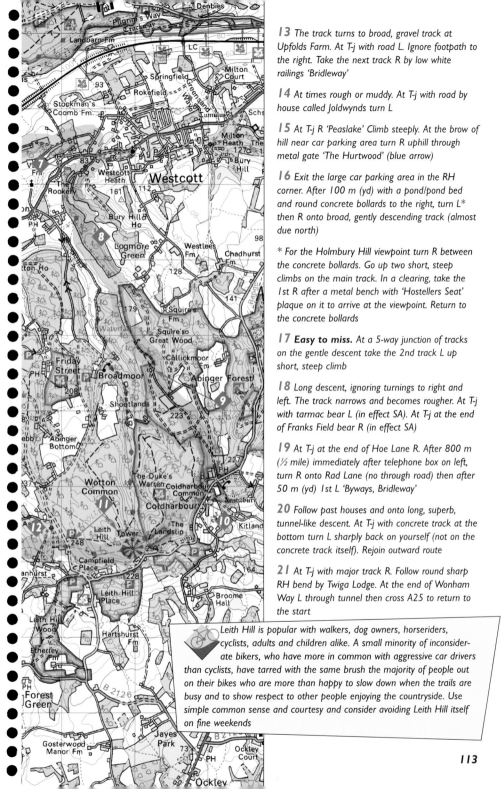

**13** The track turns to broad, gravel track at Upfolds Farm. At T-j with road L. Ignore footpath to the right. Take the next track R by low white railings 'Bridleway'

**14** At times rough or muddy. At T-j with road by house called Joldwynds turn L

**15** At T-j R 'Peaslake' Climb steeply. At the brow of hill near car parking area turn R uphill through metal gate 'The Hurtwood' (blue arrow)

**16** Exit the large car parking area in the RH corner. After 100 m (yd) with a pond/pond bed and round concrete bollards to the right, turn L* then R onto broad, gently descending track (almost due north)

*For the Holmbury Hill viewpoint turn R between the concrete bollards. Go up two short, steep climbs on the main track. In a clearing, take the 1st R after a metal bench with 'Hostellers Seat' plaque on it to arrive at the viewpoint. Return to the concrete bollards

**17** **Easy to miss.** At a 5-way junction of tracks on the gentle descent take the 2nd track L up short, steep climb

**18** Long descent, ignoring turnings to right and left. The track narrows and becomes rougher. At T-j with tarmac bear L (in effect SA). At T-j at the end of Franks Field bear R (in effect SA)

**19** At T-j at the end of Hoe Lane R. After 800 m (½ mile) immediately after telephone box on left, turn R onto Rad Lane (no through road) then after 50 m (yd) 1st L 'Byways, Bridleway'

**20** Follow past houses and onto long, superb, tunnel-like descent. At T-j with concrete track at the bottom turn L sharply back on yourself (not on the concrete track itself). Rejoin outward route

**21** At T-j with major track R. Follow round sharp RH bend by Twiga Lodge. At the end of Wonham Way L through tunnel then cross A25 to return to the start

Leith Hill is popular with walkers, dog owners, horseriders, cyclists, adults and children alike. A small minority of inconsiderate bikers, who have more in common with aggressive car drivers than cyclists, have tarred with the same brush the majority of people out on their bikes who are more than happy to slow down when the trails are busy and to show respect to other people enjoying the countryside. Use simple common sense and courtesy and consider avoiding Leith Hill itself on fine weekends

# 4 Into the Surrey woodlands south from Gomshall

**B**etween Guildford and Dorking, a few kilometres either side of the A248 and A25, lies an area of heathland and woodland criss-crossed by bridleways and Roads Used as Public Paths (RUPPs) that offer, together with the Chilterns, some of the finest off-road cycling close to London. Although some of the sections of bridleway are short, it is possible to link them via quiet lanes and so almost entirely avoid the busy roads that you expect to find in the built-up southeast. This ride explores the sandy woodlands to the south of the A25. To the north lies the course of the North Downs Way, running over the escarpment of chalk and clay, which can provide excellent or atrocious riding conditions in equal measure. This ride climbs to over 210 m (700 ft) through Winterfold Wood, with the option of a side trip to walk to the top of Pitch Hill for some panoramic views.

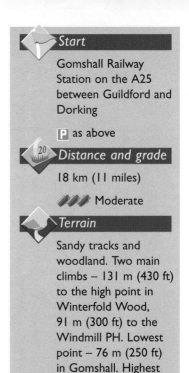

**Start**

Gomshall Railway Station on the A25 between Guildford and Dorking

P as above

**Distance and grade**

18 km (11 miles)

Moderate

**Terrain**

Sandy tracks and woodland. Two main climbs – 131 m (430 ft) to the high point in Winterfold Wood, 91 m (300 ft) to the Windmill PH. Lowest point – 76 m (250 ft) in Gomshall. Highest point – 215 m (705 ft) at the Windmill PH beneath Pitch Hill

**Nearest railway**

Gomshall

### Gomshall 1

Famous for its watercress beds and a tannery dating back at least to the 11th century

### The North Downs Way 1

Opened in 1978, this long distance trail stretches for 226 km (141 miles) from Farnham in Surrey to Dover following the line of the chalk escarpment. With regard to its off-road cycling potential, its status, unlike the South Downs Way, is not all bridleway, so you need to check a map to ensure you are not riding on a footpath. Even so, those sections where it is legally permitted to ride can often suffer from 'clay syndrome' – sticky and unrideable in winter and baked into con-crete-hard corrugations in summer. You have been warned...

### Shere 3

A tranquil village on the River Tilling bourne under the North Downs. It has pretty, old cottages with black and white half-timbering and overhanging first storeys. The lych gate, designed by Sir Edwin Lutyens in 1902, leads to the Church of St James (dating from 1190) with Norman tower and characteristic pointed arches of Early English style. A mile west, the tree-encircled water of Silent Pool is where King John is said to have alarmed a bathing peasant girl who panicked, slipped and drowned

## Refreshments:

Plenty of choice in **Gomshall**
White Horse PH 🍴🍴, **Shere**
King William IV PH 🍴🍴,
**Albury Heath** (just off the route)
Windmill PH 🍴, **Pitch Hill**

▲ Gomshall

**1** From the station, cross over the A25, turn L through the pedestrian tunnel beneath the bridge then 1st R onto Wonham Way. After 300 m (yd) on sharp LH bend by Twiga Lodge turn R onto track

**2** At T-j with road R through tunnel then at T-j L. On sharp LH bend after 200 m (yd) bear R by a triangle of grass then SA onto Gravelpits Lane between fence and stone wall. Shortly, R onto track after Gravelpits Cottages and alongside Gravelpits Farmhouse

**3** At X-roads with Shere Lane SA onto Pathfields (a tarmac lane). Climb past houses. On a sharp LH bend SA onto narrow track between fences

**4** At junction of tracks by a wooden post bear L then after 50 m (yd) take the second L. At T-j with road SA onto bridleway

**5** At T-j of tracks L over the railway crossing then R onto tarmac lane alongside houses

**6** At tarmac by Dilton Farm bear R. Climb this sunken tarmac lane. After 1 km (¾ mile) at a triangle of grass with trees turn L then immediately L again past Lockhurst Hatch on broad stone-based track

**7** At fork of tracks with a yellow stone house ahead bear R on the lower track towards a wooden barrier

**8** At T-j with major forestry track R then L 'Bridleway' (Blue arrow)

**9** Climb on track with roots showing through. At next X-roads with forestry track by small stone-built water tank SA 'Bridleway'. At 3rd X-roads SA ('Private' signs to right and left)

**10** At T-j of tracks bear L and continue in the same direction. At T-j with road L then R 'Private Drive to house only'

**11** Stony descent which improves near to a large red-brick, red-tiled house. Follow this main track as it swings around the buildings of Winterfold Farm

**12** At T-j with road turn L and climb steeply. Ignore the 1st right to Wethersell Farm. Take the next R onto tarmac lane 'Bridleway'

**13** At T-j with road near to Windmill Inn L then R into Hurtwood Control CP car park. Immediately bear L. (There are fabulous views if you climb steeply to the top of Pitch Hill but the right of way from the car park is a footpath, so if you want to go to the top, lock your bike and walk up. **NB** The bridleway from opposite the pub is exceedingly steep and it is not worth the effort of pushing your bike up here)

**14** Through the car park At fork after 400 m (yd) bear L

**15** At T-j with road at the end of Peaslake car park turn R then first road L by the Hurtwood Inn onto Pond Lane. Take the 2nd R down Jesses Lane

**16** At T-j at the end of Jesses Lane L 'Shere'. After 50 m (yd) 1st R 'Footpath' then R again 'Bridleway'. After 150 m (yd) follow the track around to the L alongside the wooden fence

**17** Bumpy section. At T-j of tracks by wooden signpost R. At the end of the track at the start of the houses SA past the telephone box. Just before the railway bridge R onto track 'Bridleway'

**18** At T-j with lane by Twiga Lodge turn L. At road (A25) L through pedestrian tunnel then R to return to the railway station

# 5 *Along the Greensand Way south of Godalming*

*T*ry this ride just to prove that you do not need to drive down to the South Downs to use your mountain bike! There is a plethora of bridleways in the triangle formed by Godalming, Haslemere and Billingshurst, and this route simply links up a few of them. Why not make up a route of your own by linking up a few others? This is a ride for old footwear and long trousers, which, despite these minor drawbacks, contains some fine views, good climbs and a few surprises.

### Start

White Horse PH, Hascombe

**P** Car park 1½ km (1 mile) north of the start at Winkworth Arboretum

 ### Distance and grade

24 km (15 miles)
Easy/moderate

### Terrain

No major climbs, though some hills may be tough after rain or in winter because of mud. If you manage the first hill, you will manage the rest!

### Nearest railway

Milford, 1½ km (1 mile) from the route at Enton

### Refreshments

White Horse PH ♥♥, **Hascombe**
Kings Arms PH ♥, lots of choice in **Godalming**
Merry Harriers PH ♥, **North of Hambledon**

Hascombe | Nore | Selhurst Common | Nurscombe Farm | Busbridge

120 150 120 120 100 80 90 80 60 120 110

0 5 10

### Bramley 8

This village has some attractive buildings including two Lutyens houses, the 16th-century Bramley East Manor in the High Street and some fine Regency and Georgian houses. A 13th-century chancel and the remains of a Norman arch can be seen in Holy Trinity Church.

### Hambledon 23

School Cottage, Malthouse Cottage and

Malthouse Farm are good examples of 16th- and 17th-century cottages; parts of the church are much older (14th-century) and Court Farm and the Granary are also interesting. The surrounding hills give good views over the downs.

▲ *Woodland track near Hyde stile*

**1** Facing the White Horse PH, take track to right of it 'Private Road, Hascombe Place Farm'. Continue in same direction beyond farm uphill on bridleway

**2** You will soon come to the muddiest section of the ride. The first 100 m (yd) are the worst and there are two more bad stretches in this climb

**3** Up and over hill. At T-j by green gate L.

**4** After 1½ km (1 mile), at T-j with road R, then 1st L after 800 m (½ mile) on Gate Street. Continue to the end of the tarmac, past farm 'No exit, Keepers only'. Follow in same direction as it becomes single track. (May be muddy, be prepared for nettles)

**5** In woodland, by signpost with yellow arrow indicating footpath to the left R, then L following blue arrows

**6** Briefly join gravel drive. After 100 m (yd), on RH bend L (in effect SA) uphill on earth track

**7** This track joins more major track near house (Bramley Park). Just past house at T-j of tracks L, following wooden fence around

**8** At times muddy (nettles). Follow track around Eastwater Barn to tarmac drive by pond. At road L

**9** After 1½ km (1 mile), shortly after fine parkland of Thornecombe House on your left R on tarmac drive opposite metal railings 'Public Bridleway'

**10** Tarmac turns to track and climbs steeply then more gently. At X-roads of bridleways near top of hill by 4-way signpost SA. At road L past large red-brick tower

**11** At T-j with B2130 SA just to the left of Busbridge Parish Council Noticeboard onto dead-end road

**12** At T-j at the end of North Munstead Lane R, then at next T-j at the end of Hambledon Road L 'Milford, Eashing'

**13** Shortly after passing nursing home on left, opposite Busbridge Lane on right L onto public bridleway

**14** Descend to pass between lakes. Climb steeply. At road at the end of the drive to Clock Barn Farm SA 'Public Bridleway, Inwood Cottage'

**15** Just before house and 'Private' sign L on track into woodland

**16** At road by sign for nurseries R

**17** **Easy to miss.** At next T-j SA onto track 'National Trust, Hydon's Ball', then immediately leave main track and turn R onto narrower bridleway

**18** Track widens. At X-roads of bridleways SA. At road R then L 'Public Bridleway, Potters Hill'

**19** Through farm, across two fairways of the golf course (watch out for golf balls!) in the same direction. At road L

**20** Shortly after Enton Hall on left L by pond 'Public bridleway'

**21** **Easy to miss.** Follow broad gravel track gently uphill for 800 m (½ mile) passing white gate of Sweetwater Cottage on the right. Just past signpost for Busses Cottage on the right fork L (blue arrow)

**22** At times muddy. At road by the Merry Harriers PH R, then after 400 m (yd) 1st L onto Church Lane 'Hambledon Church'

**23** Bear R by church through parking area 'Public bridleway'

**24** At T-j with broader track R (red arrow), then immediately L steeply uphill onto narrow sunken track. After 200 m (yd) take LH, higher fork (ignore signpost pointing down to the right). This section may be overgrown

**25** Follow through woodland then RH edge of field (good views to right). Descend through woodland to road

**26** At road R, then L 'Public bridleway'. Follow main track over X-roads of tracks

**27** Follow broad gravel track down to small road and turn R. At T-j with B2130 R to return to White Horse PH

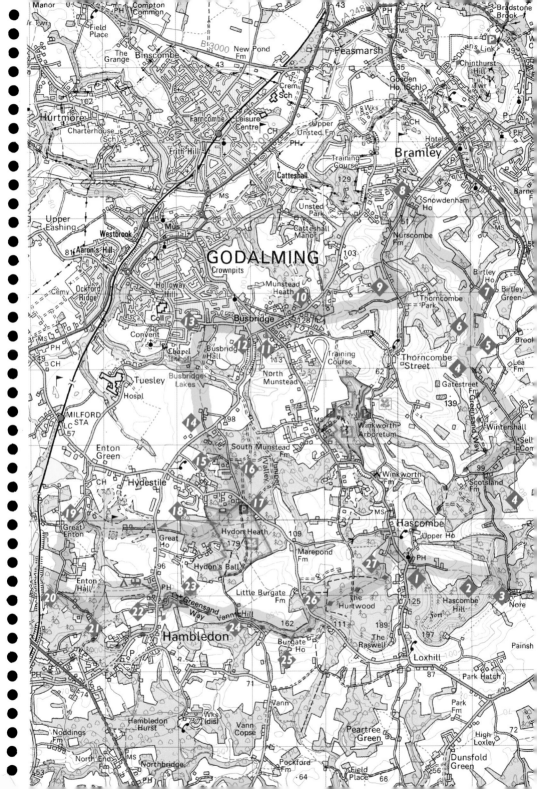

# 6 *Through sandy hills southwest of Liphook*

**Start**

Liphook railway station

P As above

**Distance and grade**

21 km (13 miles)

Moderate

**Terrain**

Sandy heathland, farmland, woodland. Two gentle climbs, one very steep 91 m (300 ft) climb from Elmers Marsh to the top of Iron Hill. Lowest point – 70 m (230 ft) southeast of Rake. Highest point – 183 m (600 ft) at the top of Iron Hill

**Nearest railway**

Liphook

**B**etween the chalk and clay of the North and South Downs, there lies an area of sandier, better-draining soil that stretches from Tunbridge Wells and Crowborough in the east to near Alton in the west. This sandy heathland can actually be at its most difficult in very dry conditions when the sand is at its softest. This tends to happen on narrow paths that are used regularly by horses. Starting from Liphook, the ride heads west past the lily ponds of Bohunt Gardens before a long, gentle climb on a bridleway of sand, gravel and flint through heathland covered in gorse and heather with fine views to the southeast. There is the opportunity of a pub stop in Rake, a village much quieter now since the opening of the new A3 to the north. The descent from Rake takes you down into the heavier clay soil, which is the bane of off-road cyclists in Southern England in the winter. This does not last for long and the route soon starts climbing through woodland to the north of Milland. A second descent to Elmers Marsh is followed by the toughest climb of the ride through the woodland of Parkgate Rough to the top of Iron Hill. From the top, there is a long, gentle descent back to the start.

Liphook    Griggs Green    Weavers Down    Rake

100    130    120    120

0    5    10

### Hollycombe Steam Collection 13

The steam age is celebrated here, amongst woodlands and gardens. Visitors can travel by steam train, listen to a steam organ and marvel at the power of a paddle steamer

 *Refreshments*

*Plenty of choice in* **Liphook**
*Deers Hut PH,* **Griggs Green**
*Flying Bull PH,* **Rake**

**Petersfield** *(southwest of route)*
Market town with handsome Georgian houses in Sheep Street and The Spain, names that recall the medieval woollen trade between England and Spain. In the early 19th century, the town was a staging post from London to Portsmouth; the Red Lion was a coaching inn. The Bear Museum and Doll's Hospital has a collection of antique toys

**Black Down** *(east of the route)*
The highest point in Sussex at 280 m (919 ft), it rises from a wooded plateau of 202 ha (500 acres). There is a nature trail through Scots pine and oak woods where deer can be seen. The views of the South Downs are spectacular. Tennyson spent the last years of his life at his summer retreat, Aldworth House, now a hotel on the east side of Black Down

**1** Out of the railway station, turn L. At T-j with B2070 (was the A3) at the end of Station Road turn L 'Petersfield, Portsmouth'

**2** After 800 m (½ mile) immediately after Links Hotel bear R onto narrow track 'Bridleway'. The bridleway joins broad stone-based track near house. At X-roads with tarmac near golf course turn R 'Bridleway'

**3** At the pond, take the middle of three gates to the R of the statue 'Foley Estate Office'. At next fork, with white metal gate to left, bear R 'Gardners Keepers, Bridleway'

**4** At Foley Hatch go SA onto gravel track, continuing in same direction on the RH bridleway along the RH edge of wood. The woodland track becomes gravel track at Stagswood Lea. At T-j with tarmac by Deers Hut PH turn L then at 3-way fork after 150 m (yd) take the middle, wide gravel track 'Weavers Cottage, Bridleway'

**5** Stay on the broad gravel track ignoring two right turns at Weavers Cottage. The track becomes sandy at Sweet Briar Farm. Long sandy/stone stretch with fine views and heather to the left. As the main track swings right to follow the line of the telegraph poles bear L to continue along LH edge of woodland

**6** At the road bear R to cross bridge over railway. Shortly take the 1st road R. At junction of roads by a small letter box and 'Oak Hanger' house, turn L gently uphill

**7** At T-j with the B2070 (the old A3) by the Flying Bull PH in Rake turn R then L 'Rogate 3' then shortly fork L onto Canhouse Lane 'Rake Industries'

**8 Easy to miss.** After 2 km (1¼ miles) and 400 m (yd) after passing Rake Industries on the right, turn L on concrete track 'Combeland Farm'

**9** At the end of the concrete track by the farm go SA into woodland, following 'Bridleway' signs. The first section may be rough. At the edge of the woodland, go through metal gate, diagonally L across field, through 2nd gate and turn R

**10** At top of the climb in a wide grassy clearing at the end of improved track bear L uphill to follow track parallel with fence at the edge of the wood

**11** At the house go SA past garage. At T-j with road by triangle of grass R then 1st track L opposite red-tiled house 'Bridleway'. At fork of tracks with a wall to left bear R

**12** The sandy woodland track turns to tarmac after house. Take the 1st track L by Wardley Cottage 'Bridleway'

**13** Follow the track in the same direction past two houses. At the road bear L (in effect SA). At T-j at the top of short climb turn R 'Midhurst 3, Linch 1' (**Or** for short cut, turn L here to return to Liphook)

**14** Fast descent. After 1 km (¾ mile) 1st road L then 1st drive/track on L

**15** This becomes a steep woodland push. Ignore turns to left and right, following bridleway signs. At T-j at the top bear R. At T-j by a stone and corrugated-iron shack bear right. Shortly, on sharp LH bend bear R

**16** Follow the main, broad forestry track as it swings to the left downhill, ignoring left turns. At T-j near to road turn R then at T-j with road R to exit Iron Hill Forestry Commission

**17** Cross railway bridge and take the next L to return to start

# Notes

# Notes

# Useful addresses

## British Cycling Federation
National Cycling Centre
Stuart Street
Manchester M11 4DQ
0870 871 2000
www.bcf.uk.com

*The BCF co-ordinates and promotes an array
of cycle sports and cycling in general. They are
a good first point of contact if you want to find
out more about how to get involved in cycling.
The website provides information on upcoming
cycle events and competitions.*

## CTC (Cyclists Touring Club)
Cotterell House
69 Meadrow
Godalming
Surrey GU7 3HS
01483 417217
www.ctc.org.uk

*Britain's largest cycling organisation, promoting
recreational and utility cycling. The CTC
provides touring and technical advice, legal aid
and insurance, and campaigns to improve
facilities and opportunities for all cyclists. The
website provides details of campaigns and
routes and has an online application form.*

## The London Cycling Campaign
Unit 228
30 Great Guildford Street
London SE1 0HS
020 7928 7220
www.lcc.org.uk

*The LCC promotes cycling in London by
providing services for cyclists and by campaign-
ing for more facilities for cyclists. Membership
of the LCC provides the following benefits:
London Cyclist magazine, insurance, legal
advice, workshops, organised rides, discounts
in bike shops and much more. You can join
the LCC on its website.*

## Sustrans
Head Office
Crown House
37-41 Prince Street
Bristol BS1 4PS
General information line: 0117 929 0888
www.sustrans.org.uk

*A registered charity, Sustrans designs and
builds systems for sustainable transport. It is
best known for its transformation of old
railway lines into safe, traffic-free routes for
cyclists and pedestrians and wheelchair users.
Sustrans is developing the 13,000 km (8000
mile) National Cycle Network on traffic-
calmed minor roads and traffic-free paths, to
be completed by the year 2005 with major
funding from the Millennium Commission.*

## Veteran Cycle Club
Membership Secretary
31 Yorke Road
Croxley Green
Rickmansworth
Herts WD3 3DW
www.v-cc.org.uk

*A very active club, the VCC is concerned with
the history and restoration of veteran cycles.
Members enjoy organised rides and receive
excellent publications relating to cycle history
and club news.*